■ ON EMPSON

WRITERS ON WRITERS

MICHAEL WOOD ▓ **ON EMPSON**

PRINCETON UNIVERSITY PRESS

Princeton and Oxford

Requests for permission to reproduce material from this work
should be sent to Permissions, Princeton University Press

Published by Princeton University Press, 41 William Street,
Princeton, New Jersey 08540

In the United Kingdom: Princeton University Press,
6 Oxford Street, Woodstock, Oxfordshire OX20 1TR
press.princeton.edu

Excerpts from "Arachne," "Villanelle," "This Last Pain,"
"To an Old Lady", "Note on Local Flora," "Aubade," "Autumn
on Nan-Yueh," "Anecdote from Talk," "Chinese Ballad," and
"Let It Go," from *The Complete Poems of William Empson*,
edited by John Haffenden, copyright © 2000 by the Estate
of William Empson, are reproduced with permission
of Curtis Brown Group Ltd, London, on behalf of
The Beneficiaries of the Estate of William Empson.

Jacket image courtesy of the National Portrait Gallery Picture
Library

ISBN 978-0-691-16376-5

Library of Congress Control Number: 2016955220
British Library Cataloging-in-Publication Data is available

This book has been composed in Minion Pro and Myriad Pro

Printed on acid-free paper. ∞

Printed in the United States of America

10 9 8 7 6 5 4 3 2 1

For Elena

◈ CONTENTS

◼ ON EMPSON

ONE

Empson's Intentions

> "What is a hesitation, if one removes it altogether
> from the psychological dimension?"
>
> Giorgio Agamben, *The End of the Poem*

I

There is a moment in William Empson's *Seven Types of Ambiguity* when he decides to linger in Macbeth's mind. The future killer is trying to convince himself that murder might be not so bad a crime (for the criminal) if he could just get it over with. This is about as unreal as a thought could be, coming from a man who seems to have been plotting murder even before he allowed himself consciously to think of it, and whose whole frame of mind is haunted by what he calls consequence, the very effect he imagines it would be so nice to do without. The speech begins

> If it were done when 'tis done, then 'twere well
> It were done quickly: if the assassination
> Could trammel up the consequence, and
>   catch
> With his surcease success . . .

Empson takes us through the passage with great spirit, commenting on every line and its spinning, hissing meanings, and then alights on a single word:

> And *catch*, the single little flat word among these monsters, names an action; it is a mark of human inadequacy to deal with these matters of statecraft, a child snatching at the moon as she rides thunder-clouds. The meanings cannot all be remembered at once, however often you read them; it remains the incantation of a murderer, dishevelled and fumbling among the powers of darkness. [ST 50]

It is an act of alert critical reading to spot the action word among the proliferating concepts, especially since it names only an imaginary act; and generous to suggest that Macbeth, crazed and ambitious as he is, even as he contemplates the killing of his king, can still represent a more ordinary human disarray among matters that are too large, too consequential for us. Alert too to see that Shakespeare represents this case not only dramatically but also through his character's choice of an individual word. But then to call the other words monsters, to identify the small verb as a child, and to introduce the moon and the thunderclouds, is to create a whole separate piece of verbal theatre, and to produce something scarcely recognizable as criticism. And when at the end of the quotation Empson widens his frame, returning to Macbeth's full, anxious meditation, he continues the same double practice. He turns our failure to grasp all the meanings into an achieved Shakespearean effect and not a readerly shortcoming, and he finds a figure of speech for the character and the situation. The word becomes a whole passage, the child becomes a fumbling and disheveled magician, and the moon and thunderclouds become the powers of darkness.

What is happening here? Empson would say, too modestly, that this is descriptive criticism—as distinct from the analytic kind. But he is not describing anything. It is not impressionistic criticism either, an attempt to evoke the feelings the work has aroused in the reader, although this is closer to the mark. Empson is tracing a pattern of thought, and finding metaphors for the behavior of a piece of language. William Righter, thinking of such effects, speaks of "narrative substitution," and of a critical style "which has the form and manner of paraphrase, but is really a caricature" [Righter 72, 68]. This seems perfect as long as we regard the caricature as both lyrical and inventive, an enhancement of the text rather than a mockery of it, a simplification that also complicates.

Empson's writing reminds us (we do forget such things) that characters in plays are made of words, they are what they say, or more precisely they are what we make of what they say, and his metaphors bring the life of these words incredibly close to us. The child snatches and Macbeth fumbles, but the child is herself a verb, and Macbeth is a man using words to keep his mind away from a deed.

I thought of this passage on the one occasion when I saw and heard Empson. He was giving the Clark Lectures in Cambridge in 1974. What I mainly remember is his waving about a piece of paper on which he had some notes, not lecturing so much as commenting on what had come up in the office hours he had held the week before in Magdalene College, the place from which he was once expelled. Much of the material was fascinating, if disorderly, but I was struck more than anything else by the energy and the chaos of what he was saying, and the sense that he found the questions that he had been asked or that had occurred to him in his conversations far more interesting than whatever he had prepared as a lecture. Recorded reports of the event come close to my memory, but have a different tone. George Watson says Empson didn't mention the names of anyone whose work he was objecting to, just said "Oh, I'm sure you know who they are." Leo

Salingar says Empson "rambled on interminably" [Haffenden II 562]. I did wonder if Empson was entirely sober, but I still felt the passion and the mind in play, and there was something wonderfully tireless about the performance, as if talking avidly about literature and life was the best thing anyone could be doing. He was trying to find his way among a crowd of ideas, and didn't know which to look at first or for how long. And I suppose I already thought that he might have his own forms of dishevelment.

For these and other reasons I see the Macbeth passage not as a model—who could follow it?— but as a spectacular instance of what criticism can do, of how personal and imaginative it may be while remaining very close to the text. If it doesn't look like much of the criticism we know, it is because it isn't.

The Empson I would like to conjure up in this book is a *writer,* both as a critic and a poet, and I need to pause over some of the meanings of the term. We use it very broadly to name a person who does writing of any kind—a screenwriter, a ghostwriter, an underwriter, even the kind of painter who is a sign writer. We use it rather obnoxiously to mean someone who makes plays or poems or novels, as distinct from a mere journalist or author of memos and memoirs. But there is another sense, one which involves no particular genre or form of writing, which signals only a long intimacy with language, a feeling that you have to care for it and can't go anywhere without it. Roland Barthes offers the clearest definition I know of this meaning of the word when he says that a writer is "someone for whom language is a problem, who experiences its depth, not its usefulness or beauty" ("Est écrivain celui pour qui le langage fait problème, qui en éprouve la profondeur, non l'instrumentalité ou la beauté"). The word "problem" may come across as a little too assertive in English, since I don't think Barthes means language is a difficulty, an obstacle in the way of meaning, although many authors do indeed think this. Barthes is saying that language for a writer is something to live with or live through (his phrase also has a suggestion of testing about it), rather than to use or admire. Of course we can (must) use it too, and we can admire it if we want to. Yet only writers (and certain kinds of reader) will believe they can never leave language to the side of any question.

Describing La Rochefoucauld's devastating maxims, Empson says:

> The triumph of the style is that he can say a very long list of mean things without your ever feeling that he himself is mean; it would not be good writing unless it was felt to

carry a hint of paradox and therefore self-contradiction. [CW 433]

I'm not sure paradox and self-contradiction are necessary, but the idea of performance is, the creation of a self in words, and certainly writing in the sense I am trying to evoke will appear only when some sort of hinting is going on as well as a more direct saying.

There is a conundrum, though. Not all critics are writers—perhaps most of them are not—and some of them are better when they don't try to be. We can say what we mean in almost any number of ways, and Empson would still have been a great critic if he had written differently, or worse—if he had not been a writer at all in my last sense. But he would not have been the critic (and poet) that he was. If his Macbeth was not fumbling among the powers of darkness, he would not be Empson's Macbeth, and we would not have this helpless killer among our repertoire of human possibilities.

II

William Empson was born in Yorkshire in 1906, and died in London in 1984. He studied mathematics, then English, at Cambridge, wrote poems and plays, acted, reviewed films and books. He left Cambridge in something of a hurry. He was about to take up a postgraduate fellowship at Magdalene College when a bedmaker discovered a pack of condoms in his rooms. The authorities inferred that Empson's plans were not exclusively academic, and, invoking an ancient local rule that sex and scholarship could not share a space, at least not if anyone knew about their meeting, expelled him.

He worked as a freelance writer in London for two years before going to Japan, in 1931, to teach at Tokyo University, where he stayed until 1934. He spent three years back in England before joining the exiled universities in China. During the war he worked for the BBC Overseas Service in London, returning to China for the years 1947–1952. He published three volumes of verse between 1935 and 1949. The works of criticism printed during his lifetime were *Seven Types of Ambiguity* (1930), *Some Versions of Pastoral* (1935), *The Structure of Complex Words* (1951), and *Milton's God* (1961).

In both poetry and prose Empson has the attractive ability to make paradoxes sound as if they were not paradoxes at all, just bits of moderately complicated thinking of the sort anyone needs to do now and again. There was a minor vogue in the 1970s and early 1980s for associating him with French theory, with deconstruction specifically, but Empson himself would have none of it. When Christopher Norris sent him some writings of Derrida and others, Empson said he thought "those horrible Frenchmen" were "so very disgusting, in a social and moral way, that I cannot stomach them" [Haffenden I 301]. He also managed, perhaps unintentionally, to invent a new Frenchman: Jacques Nerrida. What Empson found disgusting was the seeking out, as he saw it, of complexity for complexity's sake, a project that was "always pretending to be plumbing the depths" but in reality was only congratulating itself on its cleverness. Above all he took it—this was in 1971—as just one more instance of what he saw as happening to the study of language and literature everywhere: the human stakes were being removed, words were let loose in the playground, no agents or intentions were to be seen.

And yet Empson's work, for all his denials, connects him strongly to all the major modern movements of criticism and theory in English and other languages—not because of his influence on them or their influence on him, but because his preoccupations are central to any sort of ongoing thought about literature. We can't tie him securely to any style or approach, but we can't get around him either: he will always be there when we try to understand the kinds of adventure that reading can afford.

Empson is often considered to be one of the founders of the New Criticism, as it came to be called in the United States, and he is certainly the most brilliant close reader the movement ever produced. But as close reading, a fabulous classroom device, became more and more of an established method, it turned less historical and less speculative, until finally it seemed unable to refer to anything other than the words on the page, or to allow the belief that those words referred to anything beyond the page. Empson conducted a lifetime quarrel with the New Criticism's idea of intention, and intensely disliked its promotion of the work of literature as a static object, a verbal icon or a well-wrought urn, to cite two cherished images.

In 1946 W. K. Wimsatt and Monroe Beardsley wrote an important essay called "The Intentional Fallacy," advancing the proposition that "the design or intention of the author is neither available nor desirable as a standard for judging the success of a work of literary art." The piece was and remains enormously useful for the ways in which it helps us to resist lazy critical confusions of life and art, and reductive notions of causality. It also reminds us of an easily buried fact: the road to terrible work in literature or any other art is paved with excellent intentions. Intention may be where things begin—although accident too is a promising start—but the result includes quite a few other ingredients. However, the phrase "neither available nor desirable," dogmatic as good polemical announcements need to be, doesn't stand up to any sort of nuanced consideration. An author's design or intention is sometimes completely known and quite enlightening, sometimes far too blunt and entirely distracting. In some cases we shall never know it but desperately wish we could. In others we are delighted that we don't. Many authors are articulate yet distinctly evasive about intention, and unconscious intentions lurk all over the place. There is no general rule here, one simply has to do the work of reading and thinking.

For Empson, though, the doctrine of the intentional fallacy, which he liked to call the Wimsatt Law, was a rule. It said we were not to think of authors at all, literature was to be cleanly separated from the messy world of appetite and argument and intended meaning. He thought the rule was the bane of literary studies in the second half of the twentieth century, and he was almost as obsessed with its noxious effects as he was with what he saw as the invasion of English and American universities by hordes of Christian critics.

The Wimsatt Law, according to Empson, "lays down that no reader can grasp the intention of any author," or with a slight variation, "says that no reader can ever grasp the intention of an author" [UB 225, vii]. Since he thinks this proposition is both nonsensical and harmful, Empson is inclined to parody it as well as simplify it, as in "a reader must never understand the intention of an author" [ES 158] or his sarcastic suggestion that a seventeenth-century audience "could not foresee that Mr Wimsatt was going to make a law forbidding them to grasp the intention of an author" [UB 104].

"We must consider the experiences and convictions of the poet," Empson insists, follow out "the main line of interest of the author"; and to tell students of literature that they "cannot even partially succeed" in doing this "is about the most harmful thing you could do" [UB 4, 115, viii]. Going out on a rather strange limb, Empson is willing to say that faking biographical evidence is "more humane than the refusal to admit help from biography, or any intention in the author" [UB 42]. He is quite sure that Andrew Marvell "would feel ashamed of what he had done." W. B. Yeats "must have loved such a toy when he was about ten years old." "It seems clear that [T. S. Eliot's] mother had refused to sleep under the same roof as the wife" [UB 7, 176, 194]. But the passion that tilts these arguments is interesting, and we need to look at a wider range of Empson's views to understand its force.

The most blatant example of Empson's breaking the Wimsatt Law is also the funniest. To understand *Hamlet,* he thinks, we must go back to "the moment of discovery by Shakespeare" [ES 79]. This would have happened when Shakespeare's company took on a Hamlet play by Thomas Kyd (or someone else), and didn't know what to do with it because they were aware that this croaking old revenge stuff was desperately out of fashion. Shakespeare would have thought of the rewrite as "a pretty specialised assignment, a matter, indeed, of trying to satisfy audiences who demanded a Revenge Play and then laughed when it was provided" [ES 84]. Still, he carried on.

I think he did not see how to resolve this problem at the committee meeting, when the agile Bard was voted to carry the weight, but already did see how when walking home. . . . He thought: "The only way to shut this hole is to make it big. I shall make Hamlet walk up to the audience and tell them, again and again, 'I don't know why I'm delaying any more than you do; the motivation of this play is just as blank to me as it is to you; but I can't help it.' What is more, I shall make it impossible for them to blame him. And then they daren't laugh." It turned out, of course, that this method, instead

of reducing the old play to farce, made it thrill-
ingly life-like and profound.

Empson's idea of Shakespeare's "method" makes
the film *Shakespeare in Love* look like a docu-
mentary, and the touch about walking home is
marvelous. Is he serious? Yes and no, but I find
it impossible to measure the respective doses. He
is serious about considering the "moment of discovery," and about the very fine interpretation he
is proposing. Hamlet does talk as if he knew he
was caught up in a terrible old play. The rest, the
committee meeting, the ventriloquized author's
soliloquy, is bravura filling in of comic detail:
critical theatre. The question is—we are talking
about intentionality after all—how comic Empson meant the detail to be.

Not very, I'm afraid, or not at all. My friend
and colleague Larry Danson recalls a talk Empson gave at Princeton in the early 1970s, on Kyd's
Spanish Tragedy. Empson thought this mysterious play could be cleared up by the assumption
that an explanatory passage had been cut by the
censor. This would be where the conspirators
were seen conspiring. Empson had obligingly
written a version of the scene himself—"I have to
invent the words," he said—and supplied it to his
audience as a handout. The invention appears in
the talk as published in 1994. "The back curtain

opens," it begins. A character says, "All is in train, my dear Ambassador." The ambassador says, "Be sure my master will show gratitude" [RL2 58–59]. After the talk, Larry, then a newly appointed assistant professor, complimented the visitor on his "clever parody" of old school critical method. Empson seemed distinctly annoyed—no parody of any sort had been intended.

In other moods, Empson was willing to admit that Wimsatt's and Beardsley's argument had "a kind of flat good sense about it, because it is hard to know how we do learn each other's intentions." But then he was adamant that this difficulty was no excuse for not trying to get into an author's head. On the contrary, it means we have to try harder. "There is no metaphysical reason . . . for treating the intentions of an author as inherently unknowable" [CV 14].

The most important thing in these arguments is an element that is present everywhere in Empson but only occasionally stressed. Understanding literature is not different from understanding anything else. Norris puts this very well when he says that "Empson's books all seek, in different ways, to make terms between poetry and the normal conditions of language and commonsense discourse," and that ambiguity, for example, "belongs to a normal, not uniquely poetic order of thought and language" [Norris 9].

Making terms sometimes means making equations, as in the passage above; elsewhere it means making distinctions, and one of Empson's rather tangled claims engages the Wimsatt Law in a truly intriguing way.

> Any speaker, when a baby, wanted to understand what people meant, why mum was cross for example, and had enough partial success to go on trying; the effort is usually carried on into adult life, though not always into old age. Success, it may be argued, is never complete. But it is nearer completeness in a successful piece of literature than in any other use of language. [UB vii]

"Partial" and "usually" make clear the practice is common but not universal, and the remark about old age is a mildly mischievous joke. But the conclusion is startling. In the very region where we might think, from our own experience, from the long, conflictive history of literary criticism, and indeed from Empson's own work, that it has always been hardest to "understand what people meant," success is less partial than anywhere else.

The reason for literature's success in this respect is everywhere in Empson's work, often lost in the noise he is making about what he doesn't like in current literary study, but finally not at all far from Wimsatt's and Beardsley's claim, or that of most good criticism, new or old. The completed work is the test of intention, or, as Empson says, "you must rely on each particular poem to show you the way in which it is trying to be good" [ST 7]. If we combine this statement with his remark that "the judgment of the author may be wrong" [ST xiv], it is hard to see what the quarrel is about. Hard, but not impossible. For the same reason that he would rather have a faked biography than no biography, Empson would rather guess at the contents of an author's mind than leave the author out of the story. This is what he says in his quieter moments: "I would not mind agreeing, as a verbal formula, that the intention of an author can always only be guessed at, so long as it is also agreed that the guess . . . should always be made" [CV 15]. And rather more loudly, "if critics are not to put up some pretence of understanding the feelings of the author in hand they must condemn themselves to contempt" [ST xiii–xiv]. Empson wants us to see literature as a kind of continuum, a viaduct from mind to mind, and we might summarize the secret complexity of his view by saying that authors' judgments can be wrong but their feelings can't be irrelevant, because they are what the work is made of. Empson, like a good disciple of John Donne as Eliot saw him ("thought to Donne was an experience"), would include ideas and arguments among the feelings—distinguishing them perhaps from opinions.

If we borrow the trope of the death of the author, we could imagine Barthes and Empson staring at each other in a mirror, without either of them knowing who the mirrored figure is. Barthes thought the author had to be seen as dead so that writing could be rescued from the tyranny of gossip and academic pedantry, and be properly read for its own sake. But then Barthes later came to see he couldn't do without the author, that he "desired" this figure, as he said, that he had to construct or imagine an author in order to trace out certain meanings, ironies for example. This was a way of discreetly letting intention back into criticism—as an invited guest rather than a police presence.

Conversely, Empson never thought of intention as a police presence, only as the fallible but indispensable human source of any writing that matters. However, the more strenuously he asserted the need for thinking about the author's mind, the more prodigiously varied and optional that place turned out to be. There are times when Empson appears to be on the way to inventing a Monty Python school of literary criticism: "we are printing what Coleridge is not known to have written, but what he at least would have written if he had decided to keep the verse which he had long before designed for this place" [CV 54]. "I would never have gone beyond the intention of an author," he says, "either in his consciousness or in his unconsciousness" [UB 40]. This is almost delusional, if not theological, like believing two or three impossible things before breakfast. Empson seems to say that he will ascribe to intention whatever interpretation he arrives at, and we see that all along he has been doing what good critics do: trusting his own sense of the words and the writer's gift.

It is his loyalty to language as a subject that connects Empson to so many consecutive schools of criticism, including the ones he detested. He would have thought Heidegger's claim that language itself speaks ("die Sprache spricht") was worse than the Wimsatt Law, but of course Empson wasn't saying that it didn't speak, only that we need to pay attention to the speaker behind the speaking, the one Heidegger has eliminated.

The centrality of language, what some would think of as its unavoidability, is what connects most of the critical approaches that came to be called theoretical in the twentieth century. Russian Formalism haunted French Structuralism, and not only because Roman Jacobson and Claude Lévi-Strauss worked together; Walter Benjamin's thinking was often, perhaps always, inseparable from the turns his language took.

Even the austere Adorno said that one could "hardly speak of aesthetic matters unaesthetically, devoid of resemblance to the subject matter, without falling into philistinism and losing touch with the object." I don't think Adorno meant criticism had to imitate art, only that it needed to find a form that remembers what it is.

With Structuralism, language became the paradigm for a method. We could understand the grammar of social relations, literary genres, historical periods and much else as we understood the grammar of our own speech. We could begin to think about its omnipresence and its curious regulatory force, and how it works so effectively without our knowing much about it or even recognizing that we are taking its orders. Lacan's "the unconscious is structured like a language" was an invitation to think of psychoanalysis in these terms, and Barthes wrote a whole book about the linguistic structure of what he called the fashion system.

Poststructuralism was equally centered on language, but devoted to the cracks and slippages of order, the imbalance and variety of usage, let's say, rather than the seemingly infinite discipline of grammar. This shift had many faces, of which deconstruction, at first a rather technical term in Derrida's lexicon, and then an alternately glamorous and reviled academic enterprise, was perhaps the best known. In the persuasive practice of Derrida, Paul de Man and other subtle thinkers, it took language not as a reminder of secret structure but as the home of a recurring crisis of meaning, a place where interpretation learned that it was theoretically endless. Of course, this claim itself needs interpretation. Endless is not the same as pointless, and what is endless in theory is often stopped easily enough in practice. We may think—I do think—that the reasons for stopping are usually more interesting than the possibility of going on forever, although then it would be worth asking whether those reasons are practical or theoretical.

In his first two books Empson anticipates Structuralism by drawing our attention to language, in and out of literature, and specifically to patterns of meaning in places where we hadn't seen them—although those patterns are always threatening to get out of hand. In *The Structure of Complex Words* Empson offers an array of theories that finally turns his title into a sort of oxymoron. The complexity of certain words as Empson explores them, the accumulation of their many meanings and uses, defies the very notion of anything as stable as a structure.

Literary critics do not currently live, as many have supposed, in a post-theory world. There is too much theory for us to catch up on. But we do feel, I think, as once fashionable names fade and mere practice continues, that what is interesting in theory will be even more interesting in the particular case. This feeling seems especially relevant at a time when the old close reading is being challenged by Franco Moretti's intriguing proposal of "distant reading," and when models of hermeneutic suspicion, of digging into the depths, are countered by eloquent pleas, made by Stephen Best and Sharon Marcus and others, for attention to the surfaces of texts. The continuing conversation is important. We would not call for distance if we didn't feel closeness had turned narrow. And if we had not got lost in the depths, no one would need to remind us of the surface.

Empson's work seems everywhere and nowhere in this crossfire. It certainly suggests, as a sort of airlift from the battlefield, that really good close reading may be just too close, not only for comfort but also for any acceptable articulation. It will see more than it can critically take account of, pick up more trails than it can follow. This is precisely what David Miller suggests with his conception of a mode of reading that "must seem . . . a tiny bit mad," and involves us in "a never-ending *embarras du choix*." Empson, we might say, whatever he thought he was doing, was occupied with nothing else.

A month or so ago, I was trying to work out the tone and implications of a famous phrase in Rimbaud, the last line of a prose poem called "Parade," ingeniously translated by John Ashbery as "Sideshow." The poem describes a set of frightening "robust rascals," young and old, who appear to be street performers.

They act out ballads, tragedies of thieves and demi-gods . . . and resort to magnetic comedy. Their eyes flame, the blood sings, the bones swell, tears and trickles of red descend. Their raillery or their terror lasts a minute, or entire months.

I don't know what magnetic comedy is, but it doesn't sound good. And then a single sentence, itself a whole paragraph, ends the poem by saying "J'ai seul la clef de cette parade sauvage" ("I alone know the plan of this savage sideshow").

I was interested in the claim to power that lies in this assertion of knowledge, but I also wondered what kind of key this might be, and whether Rimbaud was mocking his speaker's vanity rather than celebrating his privilege. I was not, as far as I knew, thinking of Empson at all, and if I had been, I would have remembered only one two-word reference ("like Rimbaud") in a late short piece celebrating the work of Edgell Rickword, an English poet and critic who published a book on the French writer. There is no mention of Rimbaud in any of Empson's major works, in his letters, or in John Haffenden's biography. Then I read the draft of an article that was part of Empson's long quarrel with the literary scholar Rosamond Tuve about the liturgical (or not) background to George Herbert's poem "The Sacrifice." Empson is refuting what he takes to be Tuve's assertion that he, Empson, "can taste a poem better with no knowledge." He says he has all kinds of knowledge.

> I claim to know not only the traditional background of Herbert's poem (roughly but well enough) but also what was going on in Herbert's mind when he wrote it, without his knowledge and against his intention; and if she says that I cannot know such things, I answer that that is what critics do, and that she too ought to have "la clef de cette parade sauvage." [SS 124]

This key is not the only key, of course. Empson doesn't quote Rimbaud's full sentence suggesting sole, perhaps crazed possession. Tuve should have her own key because she is not a critic if she hasn't. And the swiftness of Empson's mind turns the savage parade into a display of traditional Christian horrors, a long way from the secular circus of Rimbaud. It does this because the sacrifice in the Herbert poem is that of Jesus Christ, whose refrain keeps asking, "Was ever grief like mine?" Still, I treasure this passage not only for what I learned again about the liveliness of Empson's arguing mind but also for the glimpse it offered of the range and ease of his references, the quick evocation of the cosmopolitan writer sharing rooms with the bluff Briton. The man who couldn't spell Derrida's name quotes Rimbaud as if he were an unruly but articulate young neighbor in Yorkshire.

TWO

The Strangeness of the World

"In the twenties, when my eyes were opening . . ."

William Empson, "Rescuing Donne"

I

I was born thirty years later than William Empson, in the city of Lincoln, fifty miles or so away from his native Howden, which is just across the border in Yorkshire. It's a small distance, and the gap in time isn't huge either, especially since upon leaving secondary school I also found myself in Cambridge as an undergraduate. Things hadn't changed all that much in what Empson called "that strange cackling little town" [CP 49].

The difference in class is larger, and is the reason I call up this personal history. Empson's manor and my back street were more than fifty miles apart in social space. The distance explains why I sometimes find Empson's work constrictive and comic, admirable and brilliant as it always is. But it isn't only a distance, because class in England is a link as well as a separator: to look at things from two sides of the same space, however large, is to share much of the landscape. And of course he might well have found my thinking worse than constrictive and comic, although he would have been too generous to say so. Was too generous, but we'll get to that in a later chapter.

John Haffenden suggests, in his wonderful biography, that the infant Empson "was quite the ordinary baby." I smiled when I read this. Just the ordinary baby in the ordinary manor house, with the ordinary governess, who later went to one of the classiest private schools in England. We may smile in something like the same way if we think of nation rather than class. Denis Donoghue tells us that "no modern poet has written so well about fright and therefore about endurance" as well as Empson does, and suggests that "being an Englishman helps."

> Politically of the Left, Empson has a Tory sensibility. . . . When Empson talks of his attitude to things he assumes that to be an Englishman with the blood of the gentry in one's veins is to be born with a sufficient morality. . . .

This is funny and accurate, but Donoghue's comment on one of Empson's poems is even better, because it is more precise and based not on social ascription but on stylistic fact. Empson writes (in the poem "Letter I"), "I approve, myself, dark spaces between stars," and Donoghue says, "You have to be an Ancient rather than a Modern to put yourself between that verb and that object."

This remark has been for me, since I first read it, sometime in 1974, a touchstone for social or national confidence in its most intimate and intriguing manifestations—we find its analogues everywhere, and it's always a matter of grammar or tone. Neither Donoghue nor I would feel entitled to approve (or not) of spaces between the stars, and Empson's placing of "myself" indicates a wonderful ease with the idea of having a right to an opinion about everything. I'm not thinking of entitlement and privilege in the critical, worried way we so often look at them now. We could just as easily speak of obligation. Language is full of such quiet stresses—there are plenty of working-class and ethnic markers too. But Empson's word order does present the perfect case of a manner of talking that conjures up a habit of thought and a whole social history.

Empson's account of his meeting with the Queen of England is entertaining in many ways. The occasion was the performance of a masque he had written for her visit to Sheffield in 1954. After making several jokes about various attitudes to royalty he says, "You are probably thinking . . . that I can only talk in this easy way because my whole upbringing makes me feel good enough class to speak to the Queen, so it is only a typical English boast." This is not quite what we are thinking, but Empson isn't waiting for us to answer anyway. "You are quite right," he says. Then he tells us that he "ended by feeling downright awe" because the Queen's "determined kindness" put him so firmly in his place: a gentleman certainly but only a subject after all [SS 229–230]. The joke was on him, and he tells it well. Still, he had to be serious about his "whole upbringing" in order to let himself in for the joke. I am suggesting that Empson's aristocratic origins are an interpretable aspect of who he is as a writer, not a determining factor. He made plenty of decisions that couldn't have been predicted socially.

Empson's confidence is strikingly displayed in the genesis of *Seven Types of Ambiguity*. At a time when most of us are trying to learn what the educational system wants of us, he was reinventing literary criticism. The story has been told quite a few times, and the canonical version remains that of I. A. Richards, Empson's supervisor in Cambridge.

At about his third visit [i.e., tutorial or supervision] he brought up the games of interpretation which Laura Riding and Robert Graves had been playing with the unpunctuated form

of "The expense of spirit in a waste of shame."
Taking the sonnet as a conjuror takes his hat,
he produced an endless swarm of lively rabbits
from it and ended by "You could do that with
any poetry, couldn't you?" This was a Godsend
to a Director of Studies, so I said, "You'd better
go off and do it, hadn't you?" A week later he
said he was still slapping away at it on his type-
writer. Would I mind if he just went on with
that? Not a bit. The following week there he
was with a thick wad of very illegible typescript
under his arm—the central 30,000 words or so
of the book. [Haffenden I 206]

Haffenden reports that "in fact, it was about
15,000 words," and René Wellek, in his *History
of Modern Criticism*, described the anecdote as
"a somewhat condescending, avuncular remi-
niscence" [Haffenden I 605]. Still, 15,000 words
are a lot for a weekly essay, even with an extension, and I don't read the tone as Wellek does.
Richards was being casual and friendly, trying to
catch the exceptional moment without turning
his student into a freak.

A large and rather acrid controversy arose later
about the use and ownership of "the method,"
not at all diluted by the fact that for Empson it
wasn't a method at all. Later he said, "I claimed
at the start that I would use the term 'ambiguity'

to mean anything I liked and repeatedly told the reader that the distinctions between the Seven Types which he was asked to study would not be worth the attention of a profounder thinker" [ST viii]. Here he's overdoing the modesty. His critical approach in the book is not a method, but it's not a free-for-all either. Indeed, the rather nervous attempts to classify and not to classify, to take his types seriously and not be trapped in them, are both funny and moving, analogous in many ways to the busy and uncertain mental activities depicted in Empson's poems.

When Empson met up with ambiguity (the practice if not the word) in Robert Graves and Laura Riding's *Survey of Modernist Poetry* (1927) he recognized a friend, even a co-conspirator. Later he said he had used the word "as a kind of slogan" and felt it had been "more or less superseded by the idea of a double meaning which is intended to be fitted into a definite structure" [CW 103]. This was wishful thinking, though, and by this time (1951) ambiguity had been living a rich Modernist life of its own for quite a while. The *Oxford English Dictionary* has a whole subsection devoted to Empson's use of the word.

Empson's programmatic definitions of ambiguity are broad to the point of bagginess: "any consequence of language, however slight, which adds some nuance to the direct statement of prose"; "any verbal nuance, however slight, which gives room for alternative reactions to the same piece of language" [ST 1]. The first of these is directly linked to poetry; the second relates to language itself. The change reflects Empson's shifting interests—he had published *The Structure of Complex Words* by the time he wrote the second definition—although the claims are not incompatible. In the early book he does want to go both ways, to open the house of meaning to every possible guest and also keep the guests under control, and I would say this double desire reflects the one consistent, fairly precise meaning of ambiguity in Empson's work: it marks the presence of a puzzle or a difficulty, an uncertainty on a reader's or listener's part. This presence is also connected to the idea of argument and Empson's opposition to "the loathsome theory of Imagism" [RL2 70], which represented poetry as a matter of pictures, not thought. Empson's idea of puzzlement often includes emotions but can't be created purely by them; to be puzzled is to be thinking. Puns are perfect pictures of ambiguity—or rather the best ones are. "If a pun is quite obvious it would not ordinarily be called ambiguous, because there is no room for puzzling" [ST x].

Empson asks himself "is all good poetry supposed to be ambiguous?" and says he thinks it
is. "There is always an appeal to a background of
human experience which is all the more present
when it cannot be named."

> I should think it surprising, and on the whole
> rather disagreeable, if even the most search-
> ing criticism of such lines of verse could find
> nothing whatever in their implications to be
> the cause of so straddling a commotion and so
> broad a calm. [ST xv]

"On the whole rather disagreeable" is the manda-
rin Empson suggesting that arguments different
from his own are not only wrong but distasteful.
However, we can grant the existence of great unequivocal lines of poetry, and still see the force
of the general claim about ambiguity. Not everything puzzles us, but we have plenty to occupy
our minds, and literature helps us both to think
better and to know when to stop thinking. Empson writes of his own poems that

> The object of the style . . . is to convey a men-
> tal state of great tension, in which conflicting
> impulses have no longer any barriers between
> them and therefore the strangeness of the
> world is felt very acutely. [Haffenden I 359]

II

Here's how Empson listed the types of ambiguity in a manuscript note on a poem:

1. Mere richness (a metaphor valid from many points of view).
2. Two different meanings conveying the same point.
3. Two unconnected meanings, both wanted but not illuminating one other.
4. Irony: two apparently opposite meanings combined into a judgement.
5. Transition of meaning (a metaphor applying halfway between two comparisons).
6. Tautology or contradiction, allowing of a variety of guesses as to its meaning.
7. Two meanings that are the opposites created by the context. [Haffenden I 605]

In *Seven Types of Ambiguity* the comedy arises when Empson has second thoughts without letting go of his first thoughts. A mild example of the mode is the suggestion that an instance of the third type "might reasonably have been placed in the fourth type." A dizzying bit of logical acrobatics tells us that "in a sense the sixth class is included within the fourth . . . the last example of my fourth chapter belongs by rights either to the fifth or the sixth." Empson's first seven chapters correspond to his seven types. "In so far as" is a favorite escape clause: "In so far as this is true, the example [from the third chapter] belongs to my fourth chapter. . . . In so far as this is true, the example [the same one] belongs in my seventh chapter" [ST 130, 190, 115–116].

These rather cavalier offers of redistribution are certainly enough to dispose of the idea of any coherent overall method of classification, but the types do represent a preliminary sorting of the copious examples Empson has for us, and they are "immediately useful," to borrow his phrase, not as analytic concepts but as fictions that give us time to think. If they are "hardly to be distinguished from each other," as he also says, this is not because they are so similar but because the examples they collect are so lively and individualized, not likely to rest calmly in a single category of any kind [ST 253–254].

It's intriguing too that the notebook entry makes no mention of either reader or writer, while in the book itself Empson manages to lean towards the reader while somehow imagining he is leaning the other way. The discussions of the first three types are all about what the reader makes of things. The fourth and fifth types also find their action and meaning in the reader, but Empson talks about the author each time: "a complicated state of mind in the author";

"discovering his idea in the act of writing." The sixth type returns openly to the reader ("what is said is contradictory or irrelevant and the reader is forced to invent interpretations"), and the seventh type actually settles on the writer, where ambiguities are found to be "marking a division in the author's mind" [ST v–vi].

These figures or agents are not really separable in a properly considered act of reading. Both are real at some point in time. An actual author (or a collective set of authors) composed the written poem or the oral tale; an actual reader (or listener) pays attention to it. Both of these figures— this is a more contentious point—are also to a large degree imaginary, or at least imagined. The reader needs to imagine the author, otherwise the poem or the tale is directionless; he or she needs to imagine other readers as well, especially in the case of older works or works from cultures not their own. But imagination doesn't have to be guesswork, it will even prove to be accurate in many cases; and language, fortunately, both responds to intention and escapes from it, as we all know from our experience of being, respectively, more or less understood and more or less not.

A fine example of the first type of ambiguity ("a word or a grammatical structure is effective in several ways at once" [ST 2]) is the line from Shakespeare's Sonnet 73 ("That time of year thou mayst in me behold") where leafless autumn trees are described as "Bare ruined choirs, where late the sweet birds sang." Empson tells us "there is no pun, double syntax, or dubiety of feeling" here, and ambiguity is just a word for the possibility of more than one meaning being suggested by the same phrase.

> The comparison holds for many reasons: because ruined monastery choirs are places in which to sing, because they involve sitting in a row, because they are made of wood, are carved into knots and so forth, because they used to be surrounded by a sheltering building crystallised out of the likeness of a forest, and coloured with stained glass and painting like flowers and leaves. . . . [ST 2–3]

David Reid thinks we should speak of "different" responses to the verse in such a case, rather than "alternative reactions to the same piece of language," and he is right in principle [Reid 161]. But "alternative" and "ambiguity" catch a mood as well as describe a state of affairs. A certain disquiet is part of the pleasure of reading this great line, we don't sit back and admire the riches. When I think of this poem I am most taken by the possibility that the choirs and the birds can be both literal and metaphorical—the birds can be birds or boys, and they can sing in the ruin or in the forest; the choir is a choir and a cluster of trees—and a real tension arises as soon as we remember the Dissolution of the Monasteries, which occurred in the 1530s, and altered the architectural face of England in so many ways, to say nothing of Henry VIII's sources of income.

Thinking of the Dissolution changes the meaning of the word "late," for instance: late in time (in the day or the year) becomes lately, a moment of vanished historical time. The poet is eloquently describing (no doubt exaggerating—he rather wittily fails to decide whether the tree he is impersonating has "yellow leaves, or none, or few") his sense of advancing age, but is this a fact of nature or, partly at least, the result of a human intervention? Is he just aging, or has he been aged? The notions (also found in the poem) of shaking against the cold, black night and death all feel different too, according to our interpretation or point of reference.

Empson has a nice example from *The Waste Land* for his second type. A lady's room is lit by a "seven-branched candelabra"

> Reflecting light upon a table as
> The glitter of her jewels rose to meet it,
> From satin cases poured in rich profusion . . .

Empson comments,

What is *poured* may be *cases, jewels, glitter,* or *light*, and *profusion*, enriching its modern meaning with its derivation, is shared, with a dazzled luxury, between them. . . . If referring to *glitter, poured* may . . . be a main verb as well as a participle. [ST 77]

He continues to unpack loaded words in the following lines (glass, vials, lurked, perfumes), describing the poetic action as a "blurring of the grammar into luxury." He notes too "that the verse has no variation of sense throughout these ambiguities, and very little of rhythm" [ST 78]. It's all luxury, and confirms Empson's definition of ambiguity of the second type: "two or more meanings are resolved into one."

In Empson's third type, "different modes of feeling may simply be laid side by side so as to produce 'poetry by juxtaposition.'" He thinks we may say this process is "not in any direct sense ambiguous," and answers that "it becomes ambiguous by making the reader assume that the elements are similar" [ST 115], making it hard (but not impossible) for the reader to get this assumption to work. Empson's example is the last verse of a great poem by Thomas Nashe:

Haste therefore each degree
To welcome destiny;
Heaven is our heritage,

Earth but a player's stage.
Mount we to the sky;
I am sick, I must die—
    Lord, have mercy upon us.

Of the last three lines Empson says the first "gives the arrogant exaltation of the mystic"; the second "gives the terror of the natural man at the weakness of the body and the approach of death"; and the third "gives the specifically Christian fusion of these two elements into a humility so profound as to make the hope of personal immortality hardly more than incidental to a consciousness of the love of God" [ST 115]. It's a fine touch, I think, that Empson allows his "fusion" to slither away into what begins to look like a skepticism about the way the mystic and the natural man are going to get along in the afterlife.

Turning to Donne's lines addressed to a woman

    O more than Moone,
Draw not up seas to drown me in thy sphere,
Weep me not dead, in thine arms, but
    forbeare
To teach the sea what it may doe too soone

Empson glosses the rich suggestions of moon and sphere, and then offers this brilliant reading of the compact plea, "Weep me not dead." It means: "Do not make me cry myself to death; do not kill me with the sight of your tears; do not cry for me as for a man already dead, when, in fact, I am in your arms," and also, "Do not exert your power over the sea so as to make it drown me by sympathetic magic" [ST 144]. As Lewis Carroll's Alice would say, that is a lot to make a sentence mean: this is Empson's fourth type: "two or more meanings . . . combine to make clear a more complicated state of mind in the author" [ST 133].

An example of the fifth type comes from Marvell's "Eyes and Tears":

> What in the World most fair appears,
> Yea, even Laughter, turns to tears;
> And all the Jewels which we prize
> Melt in these pendants of the Eyes.

"The chief impression here surely," Empson comments, "is not one of neatness but of parts which do not quite fit; and since the verse 'carries it off' with such an air of gracious achievement the mind is blurred and puzzled into a reflective state" [ST 172]. Is this a case of the author "discovering his idea in the act of writing, or not holding it all in his mind at once" [ST 155], as the definition of the type proposes? It seems more likely that the happily blurred and puzzled mind here is the reader's—the poet made up his mind some time ago about how exactly to create such an effect.

Among his cases of the sixth type of ambiguity Empson includes a famous speech of Othello's, and makes what must be among the most brilliant commentaries ever on the possibilities of the word "it"—hard even to see what the competition would look like.

> It is the Cause, it is the Cause (my soul),
> Let me not name it to you, you chaste Starres,
> It is the Cause. Yet Ile not shed her blood,
> Nor scarre that whiter skin of hers, then Snow,
> And smooth as Monumental Alabaster.

Empson tells us an actor should stress both "it" and "cause," and that if he himself was guessing at a one-word referent, he would say "it" was blood.

> But it is no use assuming . . . that one cause can be assigned, and one thing it is the cause of. There is no primary meaning for lack of information, and secondary meaning, therefore, holds the focus of consciousness, that we are listening to a mind withdrawn upon itself, and baffled by its own agonies. As primary meanings of *it,* however, thus thrust back among the assumptions, one might list his blackness, as causing her defection; the universality of human lust (in both him and her), as causing her defection and his murder; her defection, as causing his horror and her death. [ST 185–186]

It is no use assuming—except when we can't help it, when we are "thrust back among the assumptions." In his later critical life, Empson was eager for assumptions, and scarcely made a move without them. But here he shows an exemplary discretion in his refusal to assert a programmatic primary meaning, and an equally exemplary honesty in his letting loose the list of guesses he can't resist.

The most compelling types of ambiguity are the first and the last: the first because it illustrates, as we have seen, "mere richness"—something wonderfully unembarrassed about that "mere"— and the last because it is so dramatic. The chapter on the seventh type culminates in a long discussion of Herbert's great poem "The Sacrifice," where "an assured and easy simplicity, a reliable and unassuming grandeur" are "achieved by successive fireworks of contradiction, and a mind jumping like a flea" [ST 226]. Does this suggest "a fundamental division in the writer's mind" [ST 192], and is Empson even proposing that it does? The answer is not clear. I have already glanced at the controversy that arose out of this reading of Herbert. Rosemond Tuve thought Empson was inventing a spurious version of the author, an idiosyncratic poet, when Herbert was simply, elegantly following an ancient typological tradition linking the sin of Adam to the propitiation of

Christ. Empson felt the tradition didn't account for Herbert's delicately wilder touches. A key article of dispute was the line "Man stole the fruit, but I must climb the tree." Empson wrote that Christ

> climbs the tree to repay what was stolen, as if he was putting the apple back; but the phrase in itself implies rather that he is doing the stealing. . . . Either he stole on behalf of man . . . or he is climbing upwards, like Jack on the Beanstalk, and taking his people with him back to heaven. The phrase has an odd humility which makes us see him as the son of the house; possibly Herbert is drawing on the medieval tradition that the Cross was made of the wood of the forbidden trees. [ST 232]

"Possibly" here should be certainly, and Tuve and Empson both seem to be right about different elements of their quarrel: both tradition and the individual talent are in play. Yet the only contradiction here, the one that has caused all of Herbert's subtle fireworks, is the one that Christianity itself was born to address and scrupulously, resolutely fails to resolve. At this point in his life Empson is willing to talk about the grandeur of the thing, and summarizes the poem as putting before us

> the complete Christ; scapegoat and tragic hero; loved because hated; hated because godlike;

freeing from torture because tortured; tortur-
ing his torturers because all-merciful; source of
all strength to men because by accepting he ex-
aggerates their weakness; and, because outcast,
creating the possibility of society. [ST 233]

Empson calls this "the most complicated and
deeply-rooted notion of the human mind" [ST
233], by which I think he means not the Christian story and not even the idea of sacrifice but
contradiction itself, when its component parts
are important enough for us not to be able to live
without either. J. L. Austin once wrote that we
may "cheerfully subscribe to, or have the grace to
be torn between, simply disparate ideals." Grace
is a wonderful word in this context, but Empson
is taking us into a darker world. Hate and torture
and tragedy are not ideals, yet we may well be
torn between them and their rivals.

III

I hope the above examples have suggested something of the verve and provocation of Empson's
writing, and begun to evoke the contours of his
first critical project as it looks now—after eighty-
five years of our learning from it more than
we shall ever be able properly to acknowledge.

Empson's criticism allows us to read further and read better, whether we take his hints and run with them or head off in quite other directions. An infinite number of directions? Not an infinite number, but certainly a very large one.

"Really, universally, relations stop nowhere," Henry James wrote, sounding like a proponent of deconstruction. The appearance of their stopping somewhere in fiction is a matter of the writer's "geometry." Interpretation, similarly, can always take another step beyond the step under consideration. The great gift to us of Empson's open sense of ambiguity is the challenge of unexplored verbal territory, of discoveries to be made, and especially discoveries of what is already there, of worlds we thought we knew.

At one point in *Seven Types of Ambiguity*, he addresses a crux of interpretation in *Macbeth*—the sense of the word "rooky" in the lines "Light thickens, and the Crow / Makes wing to th' Rookie Wood." Empson tells us he would like to believe that some of his readers "will have shared the excitement with which [this chapter] was written, will have felt that it casts a new light on the very nature of language, and must either be all nonsense or very startling and new." Well, neither, because "a glance at an annotated edition of Shakespeare . . . will be enough to dispel this generous illusion; most of what I find to say about Shakespeare has been copied out of the Arden text." He is just "using in a different way the material that three centuries of scholars have collected" [ST 80–81]. Ah yes, a different way. He has replaced what used to be "or" by a magnificent assembly of "ands." "Rooky," for example, does not mean, as the earlier editors say, murky *or* dusky *or* damp *or* misty *or* steamy *or* gloomy, *or* having to do with rooks. It means all of these things. "There is no doubt how such a note acts," Empson asserts.

> It makes you bear in mind all the meanings it puts forward. . . . I feel as if one was told elsewhere in the text, perhaps by the word *thickens*, or by the queer hollow vowels of *rooky wood*, that the wood was dark and misty; but *rooky* . . . merely suggests "built over by rooks; where the other rooks are; where this rook will perch." [ST 82]

It's engaging that Empson himself, with his "but," almost slips back into the logic he is busy wrecking, and indeed he admitted a page earlier that he has "usually said 'either . . . or' when meaning 'both . . . and.'" Still, there is no mistaking the radical nature of his new intention. Ambiguity as I am suggesting we understand it—as the simultaneous presence of many meanings, a condition inflected by Empson's particular compound of puzzlement, disquiet and vivid pleasure—is the perfect complement to a whole set of Modernist developments in poetry, painting, fiction, film theory, psychoanalysis, linguistics, philosophy, and physics. Empson's own remark in *Seven Types* makes one of these connections. "Here [in the question of multiple meanings] as in recent atomic physics there is a shift in progress, which tends to attach the notion of a probability to the natural object rather than to the fallibility of the human mind" [ST 81]. To take an instance that has become very famous since Empson wrote these words, Schrödinger's cat is at one point both dead and alive but its condition has nothing to do with any subjective difficulties we may have in telling the difference between life and death.

Empson's distaste for the Symbolist aspects of Modernism can thus be turned against him. He thought Mallarmé and his followers were too polite to be interesting, and were completely opposed to the idea of argument in poetry: "Mallarmé would consider it vulgar to argue, if ever confronted with argufying in poetry, whereas Donne did it all the time. . . ." It's true that much bad poetry "consists only of a collage of logically unrelated images" [A 170]—much bad painting too. But a lot of extremely good Modernist poetry and painting might well be said to consist of a collage of images (and arguments) related to each other by unfamiliar logics. The new logic—"and" for "or," say, as in Empson's reading of the Arden edition of *Macbeth*—is the source of a new interpretative energy. This is what we mean by parataxis: not the absence of syntax but syntax's invisible twin, a relation of elements that is either implicit or still to be found.

IV

During his first year in Japan Empson visited two Buddhist temples near Nara and was much taken with the eighth-century sculptures there. Soon after that he went to Korea and China to look at other ancient figures, and began work on a book about the Buddha's faces. Much of the writing was done by 1933—in September of that year he told his teacher I. A. Richards that he had "smacked out a lot of words . . . about Far Eastern Buddhas" [SL 69]. On the way back to England in 1934 he visited other celebrated sites, and continued to work sporadically on his typescript. He wrote that he was "in no way expert in this very technical field" but had nevertheless "looked at Buddha all right, in Japan, Korea, China, Indochina, Burma, India, Ceylon and the United States" [FB 3].

The book was probably completed in 1947, and this is where its history turns into a mixture of mischance, legend and belated good fortune. When Empson returned to China he left his typescript with his friend John Davenport, who thought he had distractedly left it in a taxi. This is what Davenport told Empson when he returned to England in 1952, and it is what Empson believed until his death. In fact Davenport had given the work to the editor of a London poetry magazine, who passed it on to a colleague. The colleague died soon after and his papers lingered in obscurity until they were acquired by the British Library in 2003. Two years later Empson's book was found among them. It was published, with a lucid and informative introduction by Rupert Arrowsmith, in 2016.

Empson wrote about the Buddha's faces because he was so moved by them as works of art, but he also found in them a type of ambiguity rather different from anything he had seen in English poetry. Not entirely different: something like a tranquil fashioning of his seventh type, perhaps, where we encounter, as we have seen, "two meanings that are the opposites created by the context." The Eastern context is not torture and contradiction, but it is not a bland harmony either. Each face—in certain places at certain times, in certain modulations of the tradition—is double, and an incompatibility in the parts has "put a strain on the unity" [FB 81]. Empson thinks we shall, not surprisingly, suspect him of finding ambiguity everywhere, and remarks that

> nobody would want to say that the method was always used; the Yumedono Kwannon is perhaps the most beautiful of the few supreme early Japanese statues, and I will do well to admit, not to appear crazy over my facial theory, that it seemed to me completely symmetrical on the two occasions I saw it. [FB 81]

The exception that proves the rule, perhaps? No, because the religion and the statues are often just not interested in ambiguity or difference. That is when they appear (to many westerners) to be lofty and smug, or take on what Empson calls "a sort of transcendental pout" [FB 26]. He wants to say that whenever the religion wishes to come close to the human it uses asymmetry in its sculpted faces. And conversely, "the asymmetrical face demands a certain humanizing of the god, an attempt to get under his skin" [FB 84]. At such moments the Buddha's face "is at once blind and all-seeing . . . so at once sufficient to itself and of universal charity. This essential formula . . . allows of much variety" [FB 6].

Empson's descriptions of the statues read at first glance like Eurocentrism gone wild, unless it is Orientalism come home to roost. On a figure in Ceylon "the straight sag of the jowl gives a Mussolini effect" [FB 24]; a Chinese saint in a London exhibition seems "so much alive that it turned the people looking at it . . . into twittering ghosts" [FB 39]. The mouth of a Japanese Buddha "seems to combine a slight willful smile with the expression of prudery, which works by showing you that it is willfully preventing a smile" [FB 77]. A smile that prevents a smile: now we are deep in Empsonland. Here are some of the adjectives he uses for aspects of his statues' faces: withdrawn, patient, childish, ascetic; strained, ironical, smug; stubborn, intelligent; steady, mild; plaintive, coy, masculine, foxy; aquiline, active, mature [FB 92, 93, 94, 97, 98]. But he is not finding these qualities in a single face, as he so often finds multiple meanings in a single word. He is finding them in clustered sets on either half of any given face.

The idea of different affective qualities being expressed by the two different sides of our faces was much discussed at the time. Empson himself invites us to look at a photograph of Winston Churchill and to see that "the administrator is on the right, and on the left . . . are the petulance, the romanticism, the gloomy moral strength and the range of imaginative power" [FB 120]. But Empson's heart is not in the schematic theory, and he points out that the views of Werner Wolff ("the left embodies the wish-image of a person, how he sees himself, and the right represents his conventional face—how others see him") and Pierre Abraham ("the left carries the marks of the contacts of the individual with the external world, and the right the traces of his interior monologue") contradict each other and are both "very slippery" [FB 85–86]. In fact, Empson doesn't believe in any of the images in play. He thinks the wish-image and the conventional face are too often the same; and he doesn't believe we should "assume that each man has only one mask and one real man just underneath it" [FB 86]. He concludes his chapter on asymmetry with a wonderfully skeptical thought that undermines and illuminates all kinds of ideas about the self, identity and religion:

> It would be an odd, but not an unreasonable thing if the profoundest studies of character in all sculptures have proceeded from a painstaking application in detail of the doctrine that there is no such thing as a character at all. [FB 106]

And this is what we find in Empson's most subtle evocations of the statues' expressions: memorable portraits of figures who have left the world and still belong to it, who combine an indifference to their own destiny with an ongoing concern for that of others. Empson insists that "Buddhist art remains impersonal" [FB 113], like the religion it represents, but he chiefly means it is unselfish, not individualistic, not dedicated to the idea of "the supreme God" as a person. The snappy prose is not the voice of Europe or the Orientalist, but that of Empson describing what he scarcely knows in a language he knows very well. The joking allusions and guesses— how does he know what counted for prudery in eighth-century Japan?—are touches of self-mockery, signs that he is not taking himself too seriously. They allow him, and us, to take the images of the worldly unworldly selves as seriously as we need to.

THREE

Large Dreams

> "Say what you like, as long as it doesn't prevent
> you from seeing the way things are."
>
> Ludwig Wittgenstein, *Philosophical Investigations*

I

It's probably more unusual to bring out a major work of literary criticism at the age of 24 than it is to write good poetry at any time, but Empson started early with poetry too. By October 1928, when he began work on *Seven Types of Ambiguity*, he had a considerable reputation as a poet publishing in university magazines. Six of his pieces appeared in Virginia and Leonard Woolf's *Cambridge Poetry*, 1929; and one of them made it into Yeats's *Oxford Book of Modern Verse*, 1936. Michael Roberts's *Faber Book of Modern Verse*, also 1936, contained seven of Empson's poems. The writer's first collection, simply called *Poems*, appeared in 1935; *The Gathering Storm* came out in 1940, followed by his *Collected Poems* in 1949.

Empson's poems are remarkable expressions of learning and freedom of thought; of playfulness, ingenuity; of anxiety turned into argument. His debt to John Donne is important—he imitated and adapted the earlier poet with what he more than once called "love and wonder" [RL1, 131, 159]. The Donne of Herbert Grierson's edition of 1912 and of Eliot's 1921 essay on Metaphysical poetry was a man who thought as well as felt. He raided the rich practical and intellectual world around him for figures and tropes, and it often seems as if there was no zone of activity he couldn't turn into metaphor. These two features—the appetite for argument and the recourse to analogies borrowed from worlds that seemed remote from what poetry was supposed to be—made Donne one of the Modernists' chief allies against Romanticism and Aestheticism, respectively. In the militant new view, the members of the former movement didn't think and the members of the latter mentioned only precious objects.

Empson certainly shared this view, but his early poems also have many markers that set them apart from those of his contemporaries. They often diverge from the word order of everyday speech ("by too much this station the air nears," "What tyrant there our variance debars?" [CP 10, 13]), not usually for the sake of a rhyme (although they do that too) but in order to stretch out a thought or elevate the diction.

They are fond of elisions, leaving out definite articles and conjunctions all over the place ("It is Styx coerces and not Hell controls" [CP 14]), and they deliver what feel like epigrams in every other line ("Lucretius could not credit centaurs" [CP 12]). Their cryptic tone makes them sound, when they are not quite working, like variety-show translations of Chinese proverbs, and they often seem to aspire to a kind of wisdom, to the arrival at an intellectual plateau from which the confusions of the world can be surveyed. Fortunately they are also very funny, and they never make it to the plateau. The aspiration is all, and may not be a real aspiration, just the intimate mimicry of a frightened person's lordly fantasy of control.

In the three poems I want to look at first, Empson's subjects are an old lady, a man's fear of the woman he loves, and what remains when a love affair is over. The analogical worlds in which these subjects are situated and discussed are astronomy, biology and medicine. As with so many of Donne's poems, and indeed of Shakespeare's sonnets, the figurative fancy all but eclipses the supposedly more immediate human case, and the wit of the poems, the slightly uncanny pleasure they provoke, has to do with what we make of the gap between the two regions. We might think, if we don't like the poems, that this is a lot of fuss to say you don't get on too well with your mother, or your girlfriend petrifies you, or you can't recover from the breakup. Or we could imagine the real-life cases are just excuses for a bit of modern baroque, the mind having a holiday among allusions. More sympathetically we may conclude that the disparity itself is a form of comment, either on how much a particular instance can unsettle a person, or how far the mind can fly when it can't stay still. And more simply we may find that the analogies actually illuminate the cases, allow us to see them as we couldn't see them otherwise.

"To an Old Lady," first published in the *Cambridge Review* in 1928, begins with a famous quotation, and we wonder straight away what's going on.

> Ripeness is all; her in her cooling planet
> Revere; do not presume to think her wasted.
> Project her no projectile, plan nor man it;
> Gods cool in turn, by the sun long outlasted.
> [CP 24]

The ripeness comes from *King Lear* and the sentence is spoken by Edgar offering desperate, banal comfort to his blinded father: "Men must endure / Their going hence even as their coming hither. / Ripeness is all. Come on." Gloucester's answer is not often quoted: "And that's true too."

Christopher Ricks does quote it, and astutely takes it as an indication of "a dignified austerity" in Gloucester [Ricks 182]. It also puts the well-meaning son in his place. Ripeness is admirable if we can assume it means maturity, but what if it is just what happens to elderly fruit? Whatever his kindly intention, Edgar may only be saying that beyond a certain point of sorrow ripeness is . . . all there is. Empson's poem quickly parades these possibilities in the phrase, allowing us to see a certain undeniable grandeur in this old lady—the poem is addressed "to" her after all—as well as preparing us for more complicated propositions. The assertion of her ripeness is just a beginning, a cagy start on a perhaps impossible approach. The lady is aging, her planet is cooling, as planets do, like gods. But she is not "wasted."

> Our earth alone given no name of god
> Gives, too, no hold for such a leap to aid her;
> Landing, you break some palace and seem odd;
> Bees sting their need, the keeper's queen
>   invader.

We should not try to take over from her, or even to help her, we shall only make a mess. It's not quite that we can't reach her. It's that our world, our order of life, let's say, doesn't allow any easy transit to her world. The line about the bees is puzzling as well as rather scary. Even when a hive of bees needs a new queen, it's perfectly possible, we are told, that the colony will kill the queen the keeper introduces. The old lady not only becomes a whole swarm in herself, she will murder any too presumptuous visitor.

No, to your telescope; spy out the land;
Watch while her ritual is still to see,
Still stand her temples emptying in the sand
Whose waves o'erthrew their crumbled
    tracery;

Still stand uncalled-on her soul's appanage;
Much social detail whose successor fades,
Wit used to run a house and play Bridge,
And tragic fervour, to dismiss her maids.

We can watch her without invading her territory. I'm not quite sure how her temples "still stand" and also empty themselves in the sand; perhaps they remain as ruins while the details of their carvings vanish into the sea. She has plenty of resources at her disposal—her wit, her "tragic fervor," her sense of what now seems archaic "social detail"—even if she scarcely has any use for them now. And the last two stanzas abandon all thought of decay or loss of powers.

Years her precession do not throw from gear.
She reads her compass certain of her pole;

Confident, finds no confines on her sphere,
Whose failing crops are in her sole control.

Stars how much further from me fill my night.
Strange that she too should be inaccessible,
Who shares my sun. He curtains her from
    sight,
And but in darkness is she visible.

Now it is only the crops that are failing. And the conclusion, a brilliant *non sequitur*, suggests an alteration in the power arrangements, a reversal of the story that seemed to be in the making. The speaker who feels a little daunted by the lady and the difficulties of making any approach to her planet, anxious not to antagonize her but inclined to patronize her because of her age, suddenly settles not on the dangers of getting near but on a nonnegotiable distance. The lady and the speaker share the same sun, but she is morally and psychologically further from him than the stars that belong to quite other systems.

The closing paradox is very compressed. The sun itself, the one they share, hides her from him; he can see her only at night. The metaphor works both ways—the lady is the moon, the moon is the lady—but not too tidily. As the Gardners say, the moon "never had any crops to fail" and the lady can't be thought of as the speaker's satellite. They suggest "part-planet (an extra one), and part-moon" is the best description of her realm [Gardner 171].

And in any case the last phrase of the poem, cunningly adapted from Milton and Pope, as Haffenden reminds us [CP 197], pulls us away from any straightforward identification. We may read it as saying the lady can be seen only when the rest of the universe is dark, and Empson certainly encouraged this interpretation. The old lady was his mother, he said, and "the bang in the last line . . . was meant to imply: 'It's only when you're in real trouble that you see the old woman at her best'" [CP 197]. There is no reason to refuse this reading, it is particular, persuasive and moving. But if we feel, as many of us will, that the whole poem speaks of the sheer unreachability of someone supposed to be close, then we shall also take "but in darkness is she visible" to mean we can't see her except by peering into the darkness that is her habitat. Ricks catches this perception very well when he says "the darkness is that of night-time realization, of sadness or despair or memory, and also of the shadow of death" [Ricks 182]. Certainly it's more cheering to see the lady as a glow in the surrounding gloom, and Empson might say the second interpretation is just irresponsible, since he has told us what he meant. Usually we have to guess at an author's intention, but in this case he's spared us the trouble.

Empson also tells us his mother didn't recognize herself in the poem—she thought it was
about *her* mother. She wasn't wrong, of course.
It's not that imperious English ladies of a certain
age are a universal category, only that family
resemblances may be, to borrow a phrase from
Sharon Cameron, "particular without being personal" [Cameron, xiii]. This is a useful way of
wondering what the word "about" means when
we use it in relation to a poem. If it doesn't just
mean "based on," "referring to," then it must
mean something more curious and suggestive:
"offering insight into," perhaps. And if the insight
concerns a world and a relationship as well as a
person, it's more than likely that a poem "about"
one single person will also plausibly be "about"
several others, maybe even many others.

Perhaps the first thing we notice about the
poem "Arachne," also published in the *Cambridge
Review* in 1928, is the form: *terza rima,* also used
in four other poems by Empson. The intricate
rhymes—the end of the second line of each stanza
provokes the rhymes of the first and third lines of
the next—suggest a mode of thought constantly
returning to catch itself up, start again and go further. The mode matches the interwoven logic of
the poem, but the easily moving three-line stanza
is mildly at odds with all the stiff binary conceptual structures: devil/sea; birth/death; one/many;

truth/seeming; earth/space. The speaker is ostensibly talking about "man" in general but is clearly, we realize by the close of the work, very anxious about the plight of the individual male in a dangerous amorous world, and perhaps making life too hard for himself out of fear. Do those elegant threes offer a freedom that no rule of two can afford? This is not quite where the poem leaves us.

> Twixt devil and deep sea, man hacks his caves;
> Birth, death; one, many; what is true, and seems;
> Earth's vast hot iron, cold space's empty waves:
>
> King spider, walks the velvet roof of streams;
> Must bird and fish, must god and beast avoid:
> Dance, like nine angels, on pin-point
>   extremes.
>
> His gleaming bubble between void and void,
> Tribe-membrane, that by mutual tension
>   stands,
> Earth's surface film, is at a breath destroyed.
>
> Bubbles gleam brightest with least depth of
>   lands
> But two is least can with full tension strain,
> Two molecules; one, and the film disbands.
>
> We two suffice. But oh beware, whose vain
> Hydroptic soap my meagre water saves.
> Male spiders must not be too early slain. [CP 34]

We are always between encroaching dominions, the poem suggests, we survive by a sort of balancing act. The proverbial devil and the deep blue sea, equally unacceptable but not otherwise comparable options for human survival, become weirdly literalized through Empson's image of the cave. The devil, it seems, occupies the land, and only the hacking out of a cave will create a space that avoids both damning and drowning. This cave becomes a model for whatever space we can find between the opposing chances that beset us (that we have invented as a supposed means of ordering the universe), and then gives way to the metaphor of the spider who lives not in the water but on its surface, "the velvet roof of streams."

The spider's versions of the devil and the sea are actual predators, "bird and fish," "god and beast." The god seems to have taken the place of man here, but humans don't like arachnids much and the poem is named for a woman whom a weaving competition turned into a spider. Ovid hovers somewhere here as a source, even if he is almost immediately driven off by medieval theology, with its fine-grained notions of what angels are called upon to do. The idea of the balancing act is still firmly in focus though, with the element of dance thrown in.

The poem now turns from the spider and its survival to the constitution of the water's surface, and by extension any easily punctured surface on which one might try to live. The water is no longer a stream but a bubble. It's a "film . . . at a breath destroyed," yet of course until it is destroyed it feels quite taut and firm. "Tribe-membrane" is odd. Empson glosses membrane as the "surface of living tissue," and "tribe" as "a unity made by mutual tensions—one part removed society would break up helplessly" [CP 222]. The bubble, or the earth for that matter, are fragile yet have a way of enduring—they fall apart not through their internal differences but when the differences that hold them together are taken away. They are flimsy, varied, colorful, exciting places: "Bubbles gleam brightest with least depth of lands."

The nervous speaker now circles in towards his real worry. His ingenuity is considerable although his logic is a little slippery. If life is a matter of surviving on a fragile surface, and only differences sustain that surface's tension, he suggests, there would be an argument for saying safety lies in the number two, conceived not as a pair to hang between, as with the devil and the deep blue sea, but as a couple that guarantees survival: "Two molecules; one, and the film disbands."

The defensive allegory is all but abandoned now. The story is not just "boy being afraid of girl," as Empson said of many of these poems [CP 116], but "boy has just thought up a brilliant reason for the girl's needing him." "We two suffice." The trouble is that the boy is still afraid, in spite of his brilliant reason, and after a desperate attempt to make the bubble metaphor consoling through the comic collusion of soap and water, he remembers where his spider fable was always leading: for female spiders sex and cannibalism are just one thing.

There is something very touching about the adjectives: hydroptic, meagre. The first comes from Donne ("The general balm th' hydroptic earth hath drunk"), and suggests a very thirsty girl. "Meagre" brings out the modesty of the boy's hopes at their best. When soap seems insatiable and water is scanty, you know you're in trouble. And best of all, even the final plea is eloquently helpless: he doesn't want not to be killed, he just wants not to be killed "too early."

Empson thought the end of the poem was "too personal beside the rest" [CP 223]. But what if "the rest" was personal in its very obliquity, as I have been suggesting: "clever boy displaces his fears into physics and insectology"? The fears only grow during the journey, and the poem perfectly shows their growing.

Like the other two poems we have looked at so far, "Villanelle" appeared in the *Cambridge Review* in 1928, and as with them its technical accomplishment becomes something like the armature of its wit. The form is quite elaborate, a version of *terza rima* where the outer lines of the opening stanza recur as the last line of alternating stanzas, and as a couplet at the end of the poem. There are ordinarily only two rhymes throughout the whole piece. It is a medieval form and was relatively little used in later periods until twentieth-century poets took it up in an embrace of what we might regard as the ironies of convention. Modernist verse often seeks freedom, in the wake of Whitman for example, but there are subjects where constriction and artfulness powerfully express the freedom that is beyond the speaker's current emotional reach. We may think of Elizabeth Bishop's "One Art," where the opening phrase "The art of losing isn't hard to master" modulates into "not too hard to master." Impossible to master is what the poem suggests, yet the troubled affirmation of a mastery one doesn't have may be a means of survival—in a poem or in life. I thought at one point that all villanelles were about loss but that the recurring lines somehow contradicted or complicated the idea. The lines came back, even if nothing else did. This does often happen, but then I remembered C. K. Williams's wonderful poem "Villanelle of the Suicide's Mother." The lines return, as the form proposes, but not to qualify loss: only to freeze it, to show painfully how immobile and unalterable the loss of a loved one can be. The two recurring lines are:

Sometimes I almost go hours without crying.
It can seem her whole life was her dying.

Empson wrote other fine villanelles ("Missing Dates," "Reflection from Anita Loos," "The ages change"), but his first work in the mode is perhaps the sharpest, making the fullest possible use of the form.

It is the pain, it is the pain, endures.
Your chemic beauty burned my muscles
     through.
Poise of my hands reminded me of yours.

What later purge from this deep toxin cures?
What kindness now could the old salve renew?
It is the pain, it is the pain, endures.

The infection slept (custom or change inures)
And when pain's secondary phase was due
Poise of my hands reminded me of yours.

How safe I felt, whom memory assures,
Rich that your grace safely by heart I knew.
It is the pain, it is the pain, endures.

My stare drank deep beauty that still allures.
My heart pumps yet the poison draught of you.
Poise of my hands reminded me of yours.

You are still kind whom the same shape
    immures.
Kind and beyond adieu. We miss our cue.
It is the pain, it is the pain, endures.
Poise of my hands reminded me of yours.
    [CP 33]

The rather sinister way in which the word "poise,"
prompted by the idea of a "chemic beauty" and a
"deep toxin," keeps promising to turn into poison, as it finally does, makes us feel the speaker is
master of his or her loss but the mastery doesn't
alter anything much. The strange poise of the
sufferer's hands, a calm in spite of burnt muscles and continuing pain, recalls the loved one's
hands, although they no doubt were poised for a
different reason—because no passion disturbed
them. Time passes, the speaker thinks of kindness, and the pain returns in the returning line.
The infection sleeps but then "pain's secondary
phase" arrives, and the poise of the hands seems
even stranger. Similarly, the safety inspired
by the speaker's assurance of the loved one's
grace—no gloating or roughness or impatience
is to be feared—just reverts, like the thought of
kindness, to the repetition of pain. The two persons have only to meet for the loved one's beauty
to stir up the poison. Nothing changes: a condition that is expressed with a truly terrible finality

in the idea of a person who is "kind and beyond adieu." The pain endures; the poise too, but that only confirms the stasis of the pain. Every time they say good-bye one of them fails to say good-bye.

II

Empson came to feel "uneasy" about "This Last Pain," a poem he wrote either just before or just after he left Cambridge, and published in 1932. He was distressed to be told that he was "praising lying and affectation, like Oscar Wilde," and that the work "recommended Posing" [CP 257–258]. I'm sure his unease was authentic, but it shows an odd innocence on his part, both about his poem and his behavior—as if he didn't know his own grand casual manner could also be a pose. The unease also reminds us of a certain bluff Puritanism in Empson, of his distaste for the showier modes of disguise, which in his later view included all forms of literary theory. The name of Oscar Wilde was never synonymous with "being affected all the time," as Empson pretended to think it was.

Empson was happy enough with the form of the poem, an imitation of Marvell's stanza and meter in his "Horatian Ode": "It's hard to use; I felt I'd managed to use it" [CP 258]. Here's how the poem begins:

> This last pain for the damned the Fathers
>   found:
> "They knew the bliss with which they were
>   not crowned."
>   Such, but on earth, let me foretell,
>   Is all, of heaven or hell.
>
> Man, as the prying housemaid of the soul,
> May know her happiness by eye to hole:
>   He's safe; the key is lost; he knows
>   Door will not open, nor hole close. [CP 52]

We can't know at once that this is a love poem, as Empson says it is, and it may not be much of one. First, we need to understand the secular theology—secular because the poem asserts that this is all there is: this earth, this life. It is not that heaven and hell do not exist in the mind and in mythology. They are forms of knowledge, negative and positive, respectively, or if you prefer, negative in different ways. Heaven is the bliss we can't have, and hell is knowing we can't have it. There is an ironic security in this arrangement. We can spy on the happiness that isn't ours, peep through the keyhole into heaven. But unlike the character in Kafka's parable "Before the Law," for example, we are spared the agony of hope and waiting. The keyhole glimpse is all we are going to get. Ever.

The next three stanzas set out the poem's "theory" and worry about it as well. The worry is intricate and comic, and carries the slight suggestion that the speaker of this poem would rather play with allusions and idioms than continue difficult thoughts. This suggestion may partly explain why Empson later felt the poem went wrong, but for me it beautifully mimes the nervousness of a man stepping out onto an intellectual limb he knows won't bear much weight.

> "What is conceivable can happen too,"
> Said Wittgenstein, who had not dreamt of you;
>> But wisely; if we worked it long
>> We should forget where it was wrong.
>
> Those thorns are crowns which, woven into knots,
> Crackle under and soon boil fool's pots;
>> And no man's watching, wise and long,
>> Would ever stare them into song.
>
> Thorns burn to a consistent ash, like man;
> A splendid cleanser for the frying pan:
>> And those who leap from pan to fire
>> Should this brave opposite admire. [CP 52]

"Whatever we see could be other than it is" is a famous line in Wittgenstein's *Tractatus*, but

Empson was apparently thinking of a closer verbal equivalent in the same work: "what is thinkable is possible too." "Had not dreamt of you" is a wonderful bit of quick juggling. If this is a love poem, then the "you" is the loved one, and the proposition is an elaborate Elizabethan-style compliment: Wittgenstein thought of many things, but he didn't think of anything as wonderful as you. Or if we take the lover's mood to be a little darker, he didn't think of anyone as difficult as you. If it isn't a love poem, the speaker may be addressing himself or the reader. The sense would then be "I'm sure we are weirder than anything the philosopher thought of but he might be right in principle." Only in principle. "But wisely" is a terse way of saying we should be careful in our embrace of the claim. It's easy to forget how limited its truth is, how smoothly it may turn into a merely wishful lie.

The central figure in the next stanza comes from Ecclesiasticus, and is the fool whose laughter is compared to "the crackling of thorns under a pot." I take it the biblical implication is that thorns are a poor sort of firewood, so it is not just the sound of the laughter that is being evoked. Empson has thrown two other references into the mix: Christ's crown of thorns and the saying that a watched pot never boils. In a very crude paraphrase of this metaphysical cocktail, then, we could say that we shouldn't confuse our foolish laughter with the crackling pains of the crucifixion, and whether we treat Wittgenstein's claim wisely or stupidly, we have to remember it can only talk, it can't sing or change the world.

The thorns keep burning in the next stanza and turn to ash, as all humans will too. In a rather cruel image, this ash is promised a future only as a cleaner of frying pans, those places from which, notoriously, people who imagine they have a choice when they don't, jump into the fire. But what is the "brave opposite" they are to admire? I think the phrase points both backwards and forwards. Backwards it glances at the fire and the frying pan: in this case both "brave" and "opposite" are ironically or perhaps merely sarcastically meant: no sort of opposite at all is on offer. Forwards the phrase looks towards the next stanza, where the smoke of hell is the screen where our best dreams are projected: a brave opposition indeed. This stanza and the next continue the conversion of the Fathers' last pain into a human promise. If the final torment of the damned lies in the knowledge of the heaven they can't have, our chance of any sort of good life on earth is predicated on whatever we can invent to counteract the unreal hell we fear. The next line has the expansive generosity of so many lines in Empson's prose and poetry. The slow rhythm and the repeated l's seem to stretch out time itself, decelerate it to a friendly human pace.

> All those large dreams by which men long
>> live well
> Are magic-lanterned on the smoke of hell;
>> This then is real, I have implied,
>> A painted, small, transparent slide.
>
> These the inventive can hand-paint at leisure,
> Or most emporia would stock our measure;
>> And feasting in their dappled shade
>> We should forget how they are made.
>> [CP 52]

The slide is real because it is modest and man-made, the small focus of a grander projection. The next stanza almost topples over into an excess of diffidence, perhaps frightened by its own conviction about what is real. The "inventive" will make their own slides, the rest of us will buy them ready-made, but can we really get from this easy access to the "large dreams"? And are we going to forget how the slides are made—isn't the poem trying to teach us both to invent and to remember we have invented? "Feasting in their dappled shade" gives the game away, perhaps. The line almost sneers at our forgetting, and if Empson is combining allusions to Hopkins's and Milton's celebrations of the variegated world and the privileges of meditation, we are about as far from hell as we could be. But if we hang on to the glance at Eliot in the magic lantern ("as if a magic lantern threw the nerves in patterns on a screen"), the tone becomes less anxious, precisely because the nerves don't appear. It's a long way from screening our nerves to screening our best dreams, and among other things the distance would be a feature of any comparative portraits we might like to make of Eliot and Empson.

So we are not to forget our self-deception, just to make creative use of it. The next stanza opens with "feign" as an imperative, and the poem closes with a complicated, perhaps not entirely convincing, but deeply moving invitation:

Feign then what's by a decent tact believed
And act that state is only so conceived,
    And build an edifice of form
    For house where phantoms may keep warm.

Imagine, then, by miracle, with me,
(Ambiguous gifts, as what gods give must be)
    What could not possibly be there,
    And learn a style from a despair. [CP 53]

Wittgenstein's claim is sustained but also very nearly inverted. What is conceivable can happen, but mainly it doesn't. This is where the feigning comes in, where proceeding "wisely" is a matter of "decent tact." We are not going to imagine just anything: only what will make us think better of ourselves and our companions and our world. This is sometimes going to involve sheer invention; we shall have to picture "what could not possibly be there." The success of our invention will be a matter of style, and it will keep our hell-fearing ghosts warm for a time. The fact that it will be an invention reminds us that we are not talking about remedies for despair, only more or less elegant modes of managing it. Still, elegance in extremity is not nothing. When Wilkie Collins reproached Dickens for his happy endings, Dickens replied that they weren't happy, only the best possible versions of events he could think of that were not incompatible with the truth. If this isn't idiotic optimism, it's an extraordinary balancing act, and Oscar Wilde is nowhere in sight.

III

Thom Gunn thought "Note on Local Flora," published in 1930, was one of Empson's two best poems—the other was "To an Old Lady," although what Gunn mainly meant was that these pieces were relatively unruined by erudition and ambiguity. Certainly it has an extraordinary apocalyptic movement in it, powerful because of rather than in spite of the poem's own attempts to deprecate it. Frank Kermode recalls hearing Empson recite the poem, and seeing him suddenly stand up in the middle, as if the close of the work required a salute, some version of the respect due to an international anthem.

> There is a tree native in Turkestan,
> Or further east towards the Tree of Heaven,
> Whose hard cold cones, not being wards to
>   time,
> Will leave their mother only for good cause;
> Will ripen only in a forest fire;
> Wait, to be fathered as was Bacchus once,
> Through men's long lives, that image of
>   time's end.
> I knew the Phoenix was a vegetable.
> So Semele desired her deity
> As this in Kew thirsts for the Red Dawn.
>   [CP 56]

"There is a tree" has the sound of a fable, a sort of botanical "once upon a time," and the shift from Turkestan to Heaven—some distance "further east"—confirms this effect. The tree is "native" to those parts but there is one in Kew Gardens in London. And wherever it grows, the tree has this curious characteristic: only fire will make it flourish. "Leave their mother" is a marvelous ambiguity. When the fire arrives the cones will drop to the ground, abandoning their parent, and their fall will allow their mother to cover herself with leaves. We can understand "wait" as both intransitive ("wait . . . through men's long lives") and transitive, the equivalent of "await" ("wait . . . that image of time's end"). And then the poem shifts strikingly from magical botany to dramatic Greek myth.

Bacchus was the son of Semele, daughter of the king of Thebes. His father was Zeus, and Zeus's companion Hera was not happy with the affair that created him. She destroyed Semele by fire, by a thunderbolt she had no doubt borrowed from Zeus himself. Zeus saved the child just in time and sewed him into his own thigh prior to promoting a second birth. So the half-god of wine, a favorite with Empson and the subject of a long poem of his [CP 64–66], was not exactly born of fire, but his escape from death into life was closely associated with it, just as the magical tree both burns and blossoms. "Semele desired her deity" suggests the woman loved not only the god but also the fire that destroyed her. She didn't "put on his knowledge with his power," as Yeats thought Leda might have done; for her he was his power. This is what the Red Dawn suggests, not just a fiery morning sky but a revolution, the end of the world we know. Or rather the rebirth of the world, as the mention of the Phoenix implies, and Empson's odd, irreverent joke spells out: "I knew the Phoenix was a vegetable." The turn of phrase is too prompt and confident, comically so. The poet is claiming to be calmer than he is, and the attempted levity makes the frightening import of the poem clearer.

The thirsting tree represents a widely held but equally widely repressed belief: that only violence will allow us truly to live, to do something with time other than mark it. I don't think this was Empson's view of history, in 1930 or at any other point. But he understood the allure of such a view, and he knew the corruption and dreariness of the world it was supposed to put an end to. This active sense of an encroaching public history takes us some way from the brilliant, anxious, personal poems of Empson's Cambridge years; it also points us towards what he came to regard, on the face of it rather implausibly, as his political verse of a later moment in Japan and China.

FOUR

The Other Case

> "My evidence should be that this reading improves the sense of the whole passage on a variety of occasions."
>
> William Empson, *The Structure of Complex Words*

I

We get a good sense of the casual complexities of Empson's second critical work, *Some Versions of Pastoral*, by looking at his exhilarating defense, in the last chapter, of Humpty Dumpty's tendentious linguistic theory. Empson tells us that when, in *Through the Looking-Glass*, "Humpty-Dumpty says that glory means a nice knock-down argument he is not far from the central feeling of the book" [SV 262–263]. The immediate effect of Carroll's joke in context is precisely the opposite, of course. That is not what glory means, or anywhere near it, and that is why we are laughing and Alice is resisting. But of course we could feel that a nice knock-down argument was our idea of a pretty glorious event, that it was about as satisfying as anything could get.

It's worth pausing over Carroll's famous passage, since a whirl of language philosophy shows up there.

"I don't know what you mean by 'glory,'" Alice said.

Humpty Dumpty smiled contemptuously. "Of course you don't—till I tell you. I meant 'there's a nice knock-down argument for you!'"

"But 'glory' doesn't mean 'a nice knock-down argument,'" Alice objected.

"When *I* use a word," Humpty Dumpty said in rather a scornful tone, "it means just what I choose it to mean—neither more nor less."

"The question is," said Alice, "whether you *can* make words mean different things."

"The question is," said Humpty Dumpty, "which is to be master—that's all."

Alice was too much puzzled to say anything, so after a minute Humpty Dumpty began again. "They've a temper, some of them— particularly verbs, they're the proudest— adjectives you can do anything with, but not verbs—however, *I* can manage the whole lot! Impenetrability! That's what *I* say!"

"Would you tell me, please," said Alice, "what that means?"

"Now you talk like a reasonable child," said Humpty Dumpty, looking very much pleased. "I meant by 'impenetrability' that we've had enough of the subject, and it would be just as well if you'd mention what you mean to do next, as I suppose you don't intend to stop here all the rest of your life."

"That's a great deal to make one word mean," Alice said in a thoughtful tone.

"When I make a word do a lot of work like that," said Humpty Dumpty, "I always pay it extra."

"Oh!" said Alice. She was too much puzzled to make any other remark.

Humpty Dumpty is partly right, of course. We can make words mean what we choose them to mean, and we do—under certain conditions. The usual condition is that we use words other people understand and use them in the conventionally understood way. We can also do what Humpty Dumpty does: take any word or even noise we like and explain what we mean by it in language that others share and understand. But it is also true that any word or expression or grunt can be ambiguous. We need to know what resources the utterer or listener has or wishes to employ to arrive at a single meaning. Alice's wondering whether we can make words mean different things is too timid if she wants a simple answer, a school rule of some kind. It is the beginning of an adventure if she wants to know how we do it, and how we manage not to do it.

Noam Chomsky once said that "it is wrong to think of human use of language as characteristically informative, in fact or in intention," since it is so regularly used for other purposes as well: "to inform or mislead, to clarify one's own thoughts or to display one's cleverness, or simply for play." Following his line of thought we could be surprised that we ever manage to communicate single meanings at all, are able to cut out all the static or interference we get from alternative meanings, lurking metaphors, unreliable idioms and above all tones of voice, heard or imagined.

Ambiguities in Empson's sense—perhaps in any sense—can have many different effects on us. They can seem rich or poor, intelligent or stupid, distracting, distressing, amusing, dangerous, and much more. Empson wants on the whole to exclude the poor, stupid and distracting ones, and there are important critics of Empson, like Helen Vendler and Laura Riding, who want to exclude all his types of ambiguity from good poetry. What is interesting about Empson's broadest definition—"any verbal nuance, however slight, which gives room for alternative reactions to the same piece of language" [ST 1]—is that it not only amply covers ambiguity, but covers all kinds of other language uses as well.

If we feel we have lost ambiguity itself in such a capacious zone of implication, this will perhaps not matter too much, as long as we retain the idea of multiplied or divergent meaning. Why should we care about these different responses? We don't have to care if we don't choose to, and sometimes such an awareness will be harmful to a particular view. If you are partisan of the right to bear arms in the United States, it will help if you remove the idea of a militia from any proximity to the phrase. The relevant sentence in the Second Amendment to the Constitution is: "A well regulated militia being necessary to the security of a free state, the right of the people to keep and bear arms shall not be infringed." An ingenious 2008 decision by the Supreme Court ruled that "The Amendment's prefatory clause announces a purpose, but does not limit or expand the scope of the second part, the operative clause." Impenetrability, is what I say. Who cares about subordinate clauses, what sort of rights do they have?

II

The governing rhetorical figure of *Some Versions of Pastoral*, even when it is not named as such, is irony—which is also a good working title for the business of ambiguity once we extend its uses to ordinary speech. Empson's view of irony resembles that of Henry James, but he has a stronger and more fully articulated feeling for its uses and range: its potential generosity and its darker, cruel moments.

Describing what he calls "operative irony," James says, "It implies and projects the possible other case, the case rich and edifying where the actuality is pretentious and vain." An example would be the style of Alice Staverton, in "The Jolly Corner," the kindest and most subtle of companions, who has in her smile an irony with which "half her talk" is also "suffused": "an irony without bitterness and that came, exactly, from her having so much imagination." James knew, of course, that the possible other case will not always be rich and edifying, and his use of the word "irony" indicates something of this knowledge.

With these subtleties in mind, it is intriguing to turn to the *Oxford English Dictionary*, which is rather unforgiving as far as irony is concerned. The book is clear and helpful about the long-term meanings of the word, but not very attentive to its more flexible implications. Or perhaps the editors are just put off by indirection in general. They give three principal senses:

The expression of one's meaning by using language that normally signifies the opposite, typically for humorous or emphatic effect; *esp.* (in earlier use) the use of approbatory language to imply condemnation or contempt.

Dissimulation, pretence; *esp.* (and in later use only) feigned ignorance and disingenuousness of the kind employed by Socrates during philosophical discussions.

A state of affairs or an event that seems deliberately contrary to what was or might be expected; an outcome cruelly, humorously, or strangely at odds with assumptions or expectations.

The editors link the first meaning with sarcasm—they don't identify irony with it but they don't distinguish the two notions either. And the unfriendly (and incorrect) description of Socrates' method, as well as the words "deliberately," "cruelly," "humorously" and "strangely," leave virtually no room for ironic speculation of any kind, or for Alice Staverton's quiet jokes. Or for the effect of much of Jane Austen's prose.

The pastoral trope, in its traditional form a matter of sophisticated persons temporarily or figuratively living the simple life, is for Empson a sort of elegant engineering of the other case. Work in the pastoral genre doesn't have to be ambiguous, but it does require us to think more than one thought; it relies on a habit of picturing one set of people as if they were versions of another.

Empson abstracts this process into its two contrasting conceptual components. It becomes a matter of "putting the complex into the simple," as he repeatedly says, of "the 'complex in simple' formula" [SV 22, 53, 140]. For him pastoral does not claim that the complex is simple, or that simplicity is complex. Each is entangled in the other, and that is why the mode is ironic. "One of the assumptions of pastoral," Empson says, is "that you can say everything about complex people by a complete consideration of simple people" [SV 137]. Everything? This is a very radical claim, and stands more or less alone in its time as a refutation of the Modernist orthodoxy, stemming from Eliot, that since life is complicated, books have to be difficult ("it appears likely that poets in our civilization, as it exists at present, must be *difficult*"). We had to wait a while until our own authors devised their forms of pastoral. There are good instances of the mode in Gunter Grass's *Tin Drum*, where the inability of Germans to weep over their past is remedied in a night club that serves everything with onions, and in Garcia Marquez's *One Hundred Years of Solitude*, where a massacre that takes place during carnival is described as if the costumes were doing the dying rather than the people. In both cases, enormity appears to vanish into a simple, displaced representation, and hovers in the mind because all we can see is what the representation so diligently does not show.

Empson's conception of pastoral does not exclude the artful shepherds in Sidney and Cervantes and elsewhere, or Shakespeare's courtiers camping out in the Forest of Arden, and any other pastoral figures we might recognize. But he does widen the remit to include proletarian literature, double plots, parallel registers in Shakespeare and Milton, the obliquities of Marvell, the politics of *The Beggar's Opera*, and the intricacies and absurdities of Alice's two sets of adventures. In other words, pastoral may occur whenever there is some sort of negotiation—as distinct from opposition or crossover—between the complex and the simple. There are many other forms of irony, but this mode is ironic through and through.

In *Seven Types of Ambiguity*, Empson says irony is "a generous scepticism which can believe at once that people are and are not guilty" [ST 44]. He is talking about Portia's behavior during the trial of the caskets in *The Merchant of Venice*. Her song seems to be giving heavy clues to Bassanio, but Empson says, "The audience is not really meant to think she is telling him the answer." Still, there is a doubt about her "honesty," and an even stronger doubt about Bassanio's, who seems to be one of the opportunists Shakespeare was so fond of. And then Empson gives a wonderful example of how we understand others by seeing not only what they (or we) might or might not have done but that they (we) have stories ready for both options:

> People, often, cannot have done both of two things, but they must have been in some way prepared to have done either; whichever they did, they will have still lingering in their minds the way they would have preserved their self-respect if they had acted differently; they are only to be understood by bearing both possibilities in mind. [ST 44]

Connecting this passage to the life and writing of Paul de Man, Neil Hertz says, "One could wish that Empson's generous scepticism . . . were as widespread as he generously believed it to be." At the other end of the scale, or perhaps just among the darker shades of the same idea, there is irony as corrosive distrust. In *The Structure of Complex Words,* Empson writes at one point of "the destroying irony" [CW 307] of the word "candid"—as in "Let me be candid about this," meaning "I'm going to be as nasty as I can." Empson cites an eighteenth-century song that opens "Save Oh save me from the candid friend." And when he elsewhere discusses irony technically, he often pictures a rather ill-attuned trio:

> The basic situation for this trope, without which it would not have been invented, involves three people. There is a speaker, "A," an understanding hearer, "B," and a censor who can be outwitted, a stupid tyrant, "C." [A 178]

This is surely too reductive and strategic, and Empson himself elsewhere shows it to be so. Think of his suggestion, in *Some Versions of Pastoral*, that "all politeness has an element of irony" [SV 230]. Or this capacious remark from the same book: "An irony has no point unless it is true, in some degree, in both senses; for it is imagined as part of an argument; what is said is made absurd, but it is what the opponent might say" [SV 56].

Still, it is good to have the harsher view of irony in mind. If we don't want to take it as the basic or key version, or even promote it over the kinder modes, we still need to recognize its existence and its long tradition. An irony will often be negative, and we shouldn't idealize the form, as recent philosophers, Richard Rorty and Jonathan Lear for example, have been tempted to do. Like so many other practices we associate with reading and the arts, irony takes sides in particular instances but is always potentially neutral, available for other uses. I would love to believe, with Brecht, that whatever stimulates thinking "is useful to the cause of the oppressed," but I am afraid that if an oppressor thinks more and better he will only get better at oppressing.

Here is an Empson-inspired definition of irony we could set beside those in the *Oxford English Dictionary*: a form of utterance that we necessarily misread if we take it as a proposition to be agreed with or contested. In Empson's words, it "combines breadth of sympathy with energy of judgment" [SV 64]. What marks all cases of irony in this sense is not so much a contrast between a meaning and its opposite as an intriguing gap between meanings. The gap is invisible if we don't see the irony, a space waiting for our imagination if we do. The gap, if we see it, is the chance of further meaning, the home of the possible other case.

III

Some Versions of Pastoral is perhaps Empson's most consistent book, and many readers believe it is his best. He himself thought he had overdone the conversational tone, tried too hard not to sound like the intellectual critic. It's true he uses the word "trick" a little too often ("trick us into feeling," "trick of thought," "trick of pastoral," "tricks of language" [SV 4, 23, 115, 136]), suggesting lightweight deceptions rather than substantive shifts or complications of meaning. But generally the double effect of high-powered thought and offhand statement is spectacular. The book is littered with brilliant epigrams that most critics would envy and with large thoughts that most critics wouldn't risk, epigrams like:

The clown has the wit of the Unconscious.

The rejection of Christ may well be a less dangerous element in the communist position than the acceptance of Hegel.

There is more in the child than any man has been able to keep.

Happiness . . . involves the idea of things falling right . . . not being ordered by an anxiety of the conscious reason. [SV 13, 22, 260, 125]

The largest of Empson's large thoughts involves a curious regret hiding in his general optimism. "Many people," he says, "have been irritated by the massive calm" of Thomas Gray's "Elegy Written in a Country Churchyard," with its invitation to accept social inequality as a fact of nature, to lend it "a dignity which was not deserved." And yet.

And yet what is said is one of the permanent truths: it is only in degree that any improvement of society could prevent wastage of human powers; the waste even in a fortunate life, the isolation even of a life rich in intimacy, cannot but be felt deeply, and is the central feeling of tragedy. [SV 5]

"Only in degree" means we have to keep trying to make improvements, but shouldn't believe they will take us to paradise. The main movement of the elegy, its all too persuasive passivity, is wrong and we need to resist it. We should not "accept the injustice of society as we do the inevitability of death" [SV 4]. But then it is entirely characteristic of Empson to find a truth in the trick, so to speak.

He does the same with a related but even larger idea—not waste but inadequacy—and lays out much of his basic thinking on pastoral in the process:

The feeling that life is essentially inadequate to the human spirit, and yet that a good life must avoid saying so, is naturally at home with most versions of pastoral; in pastoral you take a limited life and pretend it is the full and normal one, and a suggestion that one must do this with all life, because the normal is itself limited, is easily put into the trick though not necessary to its power. [SV 114–115]

We have seen a relative of this proposition in the poem "This Last Pain," but here the tension is greater: the good life is not good enough, but it is not as bad as it would be if we didn't know how to pretend it was better. The claim is complicated in description, but it points to something we do quite easily all the time, and we could say this was Empson's moral territory par excellence.

All seven chapters of *Some Versions* have their surprises, and indeed all have one recurring surprise: how could *this* be a form of pastoral? The question doesn't hold us up for long, since Empson's answer is complete and inventive in each case, but it does make us wonder whether we knew that criticism could do this kind of thing. The chapter called "Double Plots" is a perfect example in many ways. It opens with a remarkable analogy and ends with an extraordinary throwaway sentence.

"The mode of action of a double plot," Empson says, "does not depend on being noticed for its operation, so it is neither an easy nor an obviously useful thing to notice." It's not alone in this respect, though.

> Deciding which sub-plot to put with which main plot must be like deciding what order to put the turns in at a music hall, a form of creative work on which I know of no critical dissertation, but at which one may succeed or fail. [SV 27]

"Must be" is wonderfully offhand—since many of us have never given a thought either to the combination of plots or to the ordering of music hall acts. But then the casual gesture goes with the discreetly democratic opening of the definition of the "creative work." If we hadn't thought of organizing a variety show, we had thought still less of programming as a form of art. But what else is it? What else is editing, for that matter, whether of texts or films? Now the world seems full of creative works on which there are no critical dissertations.

The last sentence of the chapter is "And *Wuthering Heights* is a good case of double plot in the novel, both for covert deification and telling the same story twice with the two possible endings" [SV 86]. This is impenetrable if you don't remember the novel well, dazzling if you do. The story of Catherine Linton and Hareton Earnshaw repeats the story of the first Catherine and Heathcliff, but because the members of the younger couple survive and marry, the repetition is incomplete and thereby glamorizes even further the stormy failures of the first story. The novel ends with the endlessly obtuse narrator Lockwood still failing to understand more than a fraction of the tale he has just told. He looks at the graves of Catherine and Heathcliff and wonders "how any one could ever imagine unquiet slumbers for the sleepers in that quiet earth." We wonder how anyone could imagine that death would put an end to the deified turbulence of the book—could fail to see that the long haunted narrative is just beginning.

Between the music hall and the Yorkshire graves, Empson's chapter leads us on a critical journey with many fascinating stages: *Friar Bacon and Friar Bungay, Doctor Faustus,* Shakespeare's *Henry IV* plays, *Troilus and Cressida, The Changeling;* the poetry of Pope, Donne, Crashaw, Carew and others. The chief, sinuous, subtly developed argument is centered on the imagining of two scenes at once, whatever the effect: "a situation is repeated for quite different characters, and this puts the main interest in the situation not the characters" [SV 54].

These situations are very varied: all Empson requires is the effect of repetition. In many cases, where high life and low life are both represented, as in the court and the tavern, or the worlds of the masters and the servants, there is "an impression of dealing with life completely." This is "palpable nonsense," Empson says, because there are too many ways in which two different scenes are just two different scenes. Still, the suggestion often works, it is "what the device wants to make you feel" [SV 30]. What is displayed, in many instances, "is a sort of marriage of the myths of heroic and pastoral, a thing felt as fundamental to both and necessary to the health of society" [SV 30–31]. The whole operation functions, Empson says, through the invocation of "certain magical ideas" [SV 69]—and here he must be thinking of magic in Frazer's sense, as a system of causality and connection that has all kinds of forms and homes, and is none the less prevalent in the modern western world because science deems it fantastic.

The technical point of entry into this territory for rational people is the language and imagery of suggestion. A suggestion is not a statement, and can't be controverted or prosecuted. To the orders of high and low Empson adds those of serious and comic (in *Troilus and Cressida* "the verbal ironies in the comic character's low jokes carry on the thought of both plots of the play" [SV 39]), human and animal (animals can't be damned, and humans wish they couldn't, in both Marlowe and Donne), and this world and others (Empson thinks that the Renaissance idea of our world's "soon coming to an end . . . implied that other worlds would not end when ours did, and this strengthened the feeling that everything was local, even the prophecies in the Bible" [SV 77]). Empson's most painful and threatening instance of compared worlds is "the fearful case of Swift," who is prey to "a doubt of which he may himself have been unconscious." The paraphrased form of this doubt is "Everything spiritual and valuable has a gross and revolting parody, very similar to it, with the same name" [SV 60, 250]. And his grandest instance is the moment when Hal, in *Henry IV, Part 1*, stands over the bodies of Hotspur and Falstaff, enemy hero and riotous companion, respectively, and addresses the dead Hotspur in language that applies differently to both men:

> When that this body did contain a spirit,
> A kingdom for it was too small a bound;
> But now two paces of the vilest earth
> Is room enough: this earth that bears thee dead
> Bears not alive so stout a gentleman.

Empson says "we are forced to feel seriously here about lines that this hideously clever author writes frankly as parody; the joke turns back from Falstaff against Hotspur" [SV 46]. If "stout" means courageous, as in the "stout-hearted men" of the old operetta song, it also means too large. Part of the terrible joke is that Falstaff is not dead anyway, but just pretending to be, so that Hal is literally wrong: earth does bear alive so stout a gentleman, he's still here. Once Hal has left the scene, Falstaff jumps up and congratulates himself on counterfeiting death in order to stay alive. Then he decides "counterfeiting" is not the right concept.

Counterfeit? I lie, I am no counterfeit: to die,
is to be a counterfeit; for he is but the
counterfeit of a man who hath not the life of
    a man:
but to counterfeit dying, when a man thereby
liveth, is to be no counterfeit, but the true and
perfect image of life indeed.

The argument is dazzling but also ruthless. Hotspur lies dead, and Falstaff stabs the corpse for good measure. Hotspur's bravado has sometimes been too much for us, but we can't want him mocked in this way. As Empson says, "the double-plot method is carrying a fearful strain here" [SV 46]. We have to laugh at what we admire, and worry about our laughter. We note that Empson uses the same adjective as with Swift. And yet the strain is part of the point. The double-plot method is not a method of doublethink. It requires really imagining two scenes and not letting either go, as distinct from pretending contradictions don't exist, can all be swept under the same comfortable or hypocritical carpet.

The other chapter I want to pause over is the next one, a study of Shakespeare's sonnet "They That Have Power." It has the unusually informative subtitle "Twist of Heroic-Pastoral Ideas into an Ironical Acceptance of Aristocracy." The pastoral effect arises through the comparison of a manifestly complex person to a simple flower, of high artifice to modest nature, and it is, as Empson says, very hard to know how to take this gesture.

> They that have power to hurt and will do none,
> That do not do the thing they most do show,
> Who, moving others, are themselves as stone,
> Unmoved, cold, and to temptation slow:
> They rightly do inherit heaven's graces
> And husband nature's riches from expense;
> They are the lords and owners of their faces,
> Others but stewards of their excellence.
> The summer's flower is to the summer sweet
> Though to itself it only live and die,
> But if that flower with base infection meet,
> The basest weed outbraves his dignity:
> For sweetest things turn sourest by their deeds;
> Lilies that fester smell far worse than weeds.

Empson writes that "you can work through all the notes in the Variorum without finding out whether flower, lily, 'owner,' and person addressed are alike or opposed." Reverting to the mathematics that were once his subject, he tells us that even a simplified calculation of the possibilities ("that any two may be alike in some one property") yields 4,096 options, so "one has honestly to consider what seems important" [SV 89]. Empson offers the following paraphrase of what he takes to be the poem's argument:

"The best people are indifferent to temptation and detached from the world; nor is this state selfish, because they do good by unconscious influence, like the flower. You must be like them; you are quite like them already. But even the best people must be continually on their guard, because they become the worst, just as the pure and detached lily smells worst, once they fall from their perfection." [SV 89]

This is, Empson says, "a coherent enough Confucian sentiment, and there is no very clear hint as to irony in the words." The irony is there, though, not in the tone but in the comparison of situations, and the question is what to make of it. Or perhaps what to make of Shakespeare's making the question so hard.

The person evoked, the individual or type of individual both concealed and revealed by the word "they," is most plausibly seen as, in Empson's words, "the Machiavellian" as the Elizabethans regarded him, "the wicked plotter who is exciting and civilized and in some way right about life" [SV 90]. "In some way": this is the heart of the poem's poise between precision and vagueness, and commenting on the fifth line Empson remarks on "the pain and wit and solemnity of *rightly,* its air of summing up a long argument" [SV 94]: "They rightly do inherit heaven's graces." "Pain" is an interesting word here and perfectly chosen. These people who have power they don't use, who move others while remaining unmoved, look like candidates for the wrong team in the parable of the talents, unprofitable servants, in the language of Matthew, to say nothing of appearing cold and selfish. "To temptation slow" is an extraordinary piece of apparent praise that might amount to an accusation of having no feelings at all. But "rightly" is not a wounded sarcasm, it is a desolate recognition that the rest of us, sentient, tempted human beings, are after all in the wrong. We just spend whatever inheritance we have. In a paraphrase that concludes the first section of the chapter Empson imagines the speaker of the poem as calling his addressee (the "you" in the "they") a "little plotter," whose "very faults" he must praise because they are a route to survival [SV 100]. The obvious grounds for moral criticism vanish into a helpless confession: "I am only sure that you are valuable and in danger" [SV 101]. Empson calls this "class-centered praise" because in addition to whatever personal feelings are floating around the poem, it is an instance of the commoner-poet flattering the aristocrat-patron—even if the flattery looks like a distressed negative verdict. Empson compares the result to that of "those jazz songs which give an intense effect of luxury and silk underwear by

pretending to be about slaves naked in the fields."
"It is the very queerness of the trick that makes it
so often useful in building models of the human
mind" [SV 98]. Empson's later offhand remark
about "the humility of impertinence" [SV 211]
is helpful here. We understand the reverse well
enough—it is possible to be exquisitely rude while
appearing humble. But only an artist of manners,
equipped with a very subtle moral sense, could be
humble while appearing to be rude.

In the second half of the chapter Empson turns
back to Shakespeare's plays, especially *Henry IV,
Parts 1 and 2* and *Measure for Measure*, where he
finds the same character, the cold calculator whom
he calls the plotter, in Prince Hal and Angelo. This
would make Falstaff the equivalent of the speaker
of the sonnet, the critical praiser, the displacer of
virtue. In this respect Falstaff represents a threat
the speaker of the poem can't hope to articulate, a
criticism that will not finally revert to ambivalent
approval. A wonderful example concerns Falstaff's
recruiting a hopeless gang of non-soldiers for the
war. Hal says "I never did see such pitiful rascals,"
and Falstaff replies that they are perfect for the job
they are supposed to do, that is, die.

> Tut, tut; good enough to toss; food for powder,
> food for powder; they'll fill a pit as well as bet-
> ter; tush, man, mortal men, mortal men.

"Mortal," as Empson says, carries a certain careless sympathy ("all men are in the same boat, all equal before God"), and an unanswerable indictment ("all you want is slaughter") [SV 108–109]. Yet the indictment doesn't stick, either for Shakespeare or for us, because in the end Hal becomes the king and Falstaff dies as a relegated old rascal, as pitiful as his recruits. The abandonment of the prosecution, so to speak, is what Empson calls a "queer sort of realism": "Man is so placed that the sort of thing you do is in degree all that any one can do" [SV 114]. Kings will be kings, we might say, but saints and drunkards don't do any better in the worldly world. Empson wants us to be loyal to "a generous distaste for the conditions of life," but not to ignore those conditions or to turn our distaste into contempt. It is at this point that he writes so eloquently, as we have seen, of "the feeling that life is essentially inadequate to the human spirit" [SV 114–115].

"The business of interpretation is obviously very complicated," Empson says without any appearance of irony [SV 115]. He does have a theory about this, and it is one I have already glanced at as a possible inference from his writing practice. "There is no reason why the subtlety of the irony in so complex a material must be capable of being pegged out into verbal explanations." Shakespeare's language "somehow makes a unity like a cross-roads, which analysis does not deal with by exploring down the roads" [SV 90]. And again: "It is hard not to go off down one of the roads at the crossing, and get one plain meaning of the poem from that" [SV 102]. But Empson doesn't state the important corollary, perhaps because he thinks the judgment of a critic's work needs be left to that critic's readers. The corollary is this: if criticism can't explain, can't peg things out in words, it can, often magnificently, show us what there is to be looked at, prove there is a crossroads where we so far have seen only a single, well-trodden track.

IV

I'd like to conclude this exploration of other cases by moving to a later moment in Empson's career and glancing at his remarkable essay on Henry Fielding's novel *Tom Jones* (1958). Here there is much insistence on irony, and this is also a good place to look if we want to know a little more about the importance of how we are "brought up" and the interest of "an ironical acceptance of aristocracy."

Tom Jones is a book that, Empson says, is usually felt to be just hearty and healthy—or at best clever and trivial—and also "frightfully English." With "modern critics," in Empson's view, Fielding fails twice: he has a "doctrine" to promote, and that doctrine is *not* "despair and contempt for the world" [UB 131]—which might just about be permissible if doctrines were permitted. Fielding is "regarded with a mixture of acceptance and contempt, as a worthy old boy who did the basic engineering for the novel" (UB 131)—that is, helped that notable literary form to "rise" as it so famously did in the eighteenth century.

Empson thinks this is all wrong. He (twice) finds a "Proust-like" subtlety in Fielding's thinking [UB 136, 145], and is even willing, in spite of his repeated excoriations elsewhere of Christian hypocrisy and ogre worship, to reach for theological analogies for the writing. There is a "radiance" in the novel, and "when Fielding goes really high . . . his prose is like an archangel brooding over mankind" [UB 133, 135]. As for the morality of the book, of which Samuel Richardson and Dr. Johnson thought so badly, Empson simply says, "I agree with Fielding and wish I was as good" [UB 142].

Empson, like Fielding, entertains "a class belief, that well-brought-up persons (with the natural ease of gentlemen) do not need to keep prying into their own motives as these hypocritical Nonconformist types do" [UB 136]. But then he is defending Fielding against cruder minds which, whatever their class, are trying to police everyone's behavior. Tom Jones, and Fielding himself, in Empson's reading, are "Gospel Christians," a type guaranteed to drive institutional Christians crazy. Tom's idea of virtue is to cover up for a friend when both of them have done wrong, because his friend's position is more vulnerable; or to relieve a highwayman of his weapon and give half his (Tom's) money to the man's unfortunate family—well, "rather more than half," as Empson says, "to avoid calculation" [UB 140].

Empson has a theory about Fielding's theory:

> The society which Fielding describes is one in which many different codes of honour, indeed almost different tribes, exist concurrently. The central governing class acts by only one of these codes and is too proud to look at the others . . . but they would be better magistrates, and also happier and more sensible in their private lives, if they would recognize that these other codes surround them. It is to make this central point that Fielding needs the technique of double irony, without which one cannot express imaginative sympathy for two codes at once. [UB 141–142]

It is one idea of honor for a single gentleman *not* to say no to any woman who really wants to sleep with him; another for a poor man to believe that it is "shameful" *not* to betray his friend if there is money in it for himself and his family. Fielding doesn't endorse either of these codes, or many others, but he does, according to Empson, want us to "gather that the confusion between different moral codes" helps to make all of them at least "intelligible" [UB 146].

And the doctrine? For Empson it is a matter of decency of moral impulse—when it exists, that is, the predisposition is not universal:

"If good by nature, you can imagine other people's feelings so directly that you have an impulse to act on them as if they were your own; and this is the source of your greatest pleasures as well as of your only genuinely unselfish actions." [UB 137]

Doesn't such a claim directly feed the objections of Johnson and others? Good people are "good by nature," others are bad by the same agency, and there is nothing the individual can do about it. All the teachings of church and family are irrelevant. No, the argument is that even good impulses can go astray, and we are entirely responsible for our actions, whatever they are. But we still need to trust something other than abstract sermons, something more practical and irregular and intuitive. Empson notes that Fielding "never defines" his doctrine "as his central thesis" [UB 134], and that he seems to feel that there is something "baffling" as well as urgent about Christian thought when taken radically. Indeed, when Fielding has Tom "carry out one of the paradoxes of Jesus . . . neither Fielding nor Tom must ever say so" [UB 140].

At this point the most helpful line of thought seems to be one that comes from Empson himself but partly contradicts his main argument. He proposes that Fielding holds and implicitly urges on us the doctrine he describes in the quotation above. I wonder whether Fielding does not rather pretend to have a doctrine along those lines, and half-reveal it, but then actually suggest that no doctrine will do, because the very idea of such a thing is too static and too grand, and moral impulses are both kinder and messier than anything a doctrine could proclaim. This perhaps makes Fielding sound too much like an author whom those "modern critics" might come to admire, but it is what Empson himself says in one of his grandest lines:

> The time must clearly come, if a man carries through a consistent programme about double irony, when he himself does not know the answer. [UB 144]

Empson's affinity with Fielding is remarkable, and reminds us that although pride in class, whether displayed by an aristocrat or a worker, usually yields only repellent snobbery, a certain comfort with the idea of class allows us to use it as a means of understanding and to forget about it in almost every other respect. This way of thinking then becomes part of a larger argument about the other case:

> It strikes me that modern critics . . . have become oddly resistant to admitting that there is more than one code of morals in the world, whereas the central purpose of reading imaginative literature is to accustom yourself to this basic fact. [UB 142]

FIVE

All in Flight

> "I wanted control over the broadcasting of any
> ambiguities."
>
> Gillian Rose, *Love's Work*

I

Empson wrote that his later poems were largely
focused on the historical theme that also en-
gaged other, apparently more political poets,
namely "the gradual sinister confusing approach
to the Second World War." Of his second book of
verse, *The Gathering Storm* (1940), he wrote that
"nearly all the poems really are considering this
prospect." He also said, partly in jest, that the title
means "just what Winston Churchill did when
he stole it" [CP 127]. Churchill's *The Gathering
Storm* is the first book in his six-volume history
of the war.

The theme is certainly present in the remarkable poem "Aubade," written in 1933 or 1934, but
it arrives very late in the poem and can't fully be
disentangled from personal matters. The story
involves two lovers woken by an earthquake in
Japan, and the initial question is whether they

should stay in the speaker's house or leave. It is on a cliff, we are told, and the weather "could take / Bookloads off shelves, break bottles in a row."

> Then the long pause and then the bigger shake.
> It seemed the best thing to be up and go.
> [CP 69]

"Up" can mean out of bed or fully awake; and "up and off" hovers behind "up and go." "The best thing" may refer to immediate physical action, or to a longer-term view of the relationship. The second stanza is a little hard to read.

> And far too large for my feet to step by.
> I hoped that various building were
> brought low.
> The heart of standing is you cannot fly. [CP 69]

What's "far too large" seems to be the tremor continuing after a pause ("and then the bigger shake"), but "cannot fly" surely represents what the speaker wants to think rather than any actual impossibility.

> It seemed quite safe till she got up and dressed.
> The guarded tourist makes the guide the test.
> Then I said The Garden? Laughing she said No.
> Taxi for her and for me healthy rest.
> It seemed the best thing to be up and go.
> [CP 69]

The last line here seems to be a form of indirect speech, a paraphrase of the speaker's nervous understanding of what the woman says. To a question about safety, she answers with a laugh and a thought about transport. The speaker is rueful.

> The language problem but you have to try
> Some solid ground for lying could she show?
> The heart of standing is you cannot fly. [CP 69]

He wonders why she wants to leave, and since he's a poet (or since he is a version of Empson), he does his wondering with a pun. The language problem may not be the obvious one, the tourist's poor or nonexistent grasp of Japanese. It may also involve the English mania for suspicion in words and of words: is the woman lying to him or telling him why she can't lie with him any longer? But both meanings of lying turn out to be irrelevant.

> None of these deaths were her point at all.
> The thing was that being woken he would bawl
> And finding her not in earshot he would know.
> I tried saying Half an Hour to pay this call.
> It seemed the best thing to be up and go.
>   [CP 69]

These deaths: the deaths that have occurred in the earthquake and the further deaths that may occur if people venture outdoors too soon. She needs to get home because someone—a husband or a child—will cry or complain as soon as he discovers she is not there.

The speaker sleeps for a bit, and the topic of the poem begins to shift.

> I slept, and blank as that I would yet lie.
> Till you have seen what a threat holds below,
> The heart of standing is you cannot fly. [CP 69]

The speaker is not ready to let go of his pun. He hints that he would be lying if he said that sleep solved any sort of problem, but also says he wished he could continue in that blankness, a condition where at least he doesn't have to worry so rationally about staying or leaving. His logic is about seeing "what a threat holds below" is strange, but also convincing: perhaps we can't (or shouldn't) fly until we've looked the danger in the face

And now suddenly the shift is completed. The question no longer concerns the earthquake and the couple, although the comic tourist and guide are still within reach. The speaker wonders whether it may be time to leave Japan, and not just this house.

> Tell me again about Europe and her pains,
> Who's tortured by the drought, who by the
>   rains.

Glut me with floods where only the swine
   can row
Who cuts his throat and let him count his
   gains.
It seemed the best thing to be up and go.
   [CP 69]

On second thought, the refrain seems to say,
perhaps I'd better go and find out for myself. Or
does he mean he should get up and go to work
today—as long as he is so far from Europe, he
should be doing the job he's paid for in Japan.
The next stanza takes him towards Japan rather
than away from it.

A bedshift flight to a Far Eastern sky.
Only the same war on a stronger toe.
The heart of standing is you cannot fly. [CP 70]

"Bedshift" is quite wonderful in its unruly meanings: it reminds us of the lovers being woken by
the earthquake, evokes a night journey by plane,
and suggests something makeshift about the
whole situation. The Gardners engagingly associate the word with magic carpets [Gardner 166].
Perhaps our man is not thinking of leaving but
remembering his arrival, recalling the uncertain
political climate of Europe, the war already in the
air. War is present in the East too, "the same war
on a stronger toe." If it really is the same war, then

of course the question of standing or flying becomes in many ways moot. Empson tells us the poem "was written in Tokyo during the Manchurian Incident," and brings the international question back to the couple: "It was thought unwise for visiting Englishmen to marry Japanese ladies, because the two countries would clearly soon be at war" [CP 316].

The next stanzas don't clarify anything, yet they have an unmistakable urgency about them, as if the real question were not about staying or leaving, standing or flying, but how one should feel about any such action, whichever one does. 'Tell me more quickly what I lost by this," the speaker says. Almost everything is unmoored in this sentence. Whom is he asking? More quickly than what? What is "this"? Let's say he is asking anyone who will reply to him, in reality or in imagination. And "this" could be the love affair, the change in it that may follow the earthquake, the whole relation between the guide and the tourist, the tourist's awareness that he is never going to be a native here. It could be whatever decision he arrives at. The poem, as if sensing that we are not going to be much help, offers an alternative:

> Or tell me with less drama what they miss
> Who call no die a god for a good throw,

Who say after two aliens had one kiss
It seemed the best thing to be up and go.
　　[CP 70]

"With less drama" parallels "more quickly"—there is a real worry about taking things too grandly, turning affective molehills into international mountains. But the "I" has interestingly turned into a "they"; a notional type takes over from a person. The line about the gambling is truly opaque and awkward, I think, but weirdly haunting. I take it we are meant to imagine types who miss something important because they pride themselves on their calm, on their lack of extreme behavior—they are not going to worship chance just because they might be lucky. And then this rather "English" common sense slips into an equally "English" habit of not taking foreigners (or each other perhaps) too seriously. "One kiss," and it's time to be off. Thank God for the reminder the earthquake provided. "It seemed the best thing" in this light is cruelly comic: can't be too careful when it comes to aliens.

The poem reaches its conclusion with a repetition of the word "tell"—the speaker is going to tell us what we can't tell him—and another pun.

But as to risings, I can tell you why.
It is on contradiction that they grow.
It seemed the best thing to be up and go.

Up was the heartening and the strong reply.
The heart of standing is we cannot fly. [CP 70]

"Risings" evokes the war situation in the East and the West, but in this context must also call up the manifestations of sexual desire, as well as the notion of getting up and going. What does the speaker have to say about these things? That "it is on contradiction that they grow." This seems obvious in the political context, less so in the personal one. But we have to believe the speaker has found something he wants to say to himself. The repetition of the first refrain—"It seemed the best thing to be up and go"—which appears to be a conclusion drawn from the theory of risings growing out of contradictions, might be thought to settle things. Since contradiction is at the heart of these matters, rising itself means leaving, taking action, even if the sexual meaning of the word implies that one has to linger in one place, with one person, now and then. "Up and go" is a rather brutally witty description of a one-night stand.

But the refrain doesn't settle things, since the apparent agreement in the next line holds only for a second. "Up was the heartening and the strong reply." "Up" without "go" might mean a lot more risings in the same place, and this is where the refrain leaves us: "The heart of standing is we cannot fly." In a quiet but significant substitution,

Empson has replaced "you" with "we." "Heartening" and "heart" create a troubling echo, almost an irony. How heartening is it to be told you cannot fly? Not quite the right question perhaps. When and for whom would it be heartening to be told this? And how do we read "heart"? Are there other kinds of standing—heartless kinds?

Empson doesn't explicitly connect "Aubade" to the Fool's song in *King Lear* about staying and flying, but the two lyrics do illuminate each other beautifully. The Earl of Kent, banished from Britain by the angry king, has returned in disguise to go on serving his master. He is now in the stocks for his trouble, and asks the king's Fool what has happened to all the knights who were supposed to be part of the king's retinue. (They are in the process of being dispersed by the king's daughters, who thought, probably correctly, that the knights were too riotous, but in any case wish to reduce the king's status, keep him in his new lowly place.) The Fool says that if Kent had been put in the stocks for asking that question he would have deserved the punishment. It's a wise fool's idea: we shouldn't punish people for courage or loyalty, only for not knowing what's going on.

The Fool follows up with an extravagant piece of apparent nonsense which gradually turns into an ironic recommendation to stick with people who are rising rather than falling in the world, and ends with the following offer: "When a wise man gives thee better counsel, give me mine again: I would have none but knaves follow it, since a fool gives it." The idea of giving counsel back, as if it were a loan, makes us wonder whether we know what giving is, and the mention of knaves is important for the wonderful song the Fool now sings.

> That sir which serves and seeks for gain,
> > And follows but for form,
> Will pack when it begins to rain,
> > And leave thee in the storm.
> But I will tarry; the fool will stay,
> > And let the wise man fly:
> The knave turns fool that runs away;
> > The fool no knave, perdy.

Kent asks the Fool where he learned what he is singing, and the Fool answers "Not i' the stocks, fool": a brilliant imitation of the self-preserving person the Fool is not.

He will stay. The last two lines offer, in an intensely compressed form, portraits of two kinds of folly: that of the clever knave who is willing to appear foolish if it will save his skin, and that of the loyal fool who refuses all forms of knavery.

Obviously there are major differences between Empson's poem and the Fool's song. The poem is about deciding to leave or not to leave, and no one is being abandoned to a storm, since the storm is going to be everywhere. It's not even clear that leaving the woman—as distinct from leaving Japan or continuing to avoid Europe—is a major worry. The character in *King Lear* knows what he is going to do, and also, by contrast, that this is what most other people would not do. The stories do meet up, though, on opposite sides of a strict fence. The figure in the poem is the reverse of a fool, he is an over-intelligent worrier, but he is right to worry, since he may just not be brave enough for folly.

II

"Autumn on Nan-Yueh" is Empson's longest and most conversational poem, the least tending towards the compression of maxim and aphorism. It displays, however, a continuing interplay between the poet's formal choices and the topics he addresses. The rhyme scheme is tight and intricate and we might pause over some of the matched words: Yeats/fates, wrong/song, despair/flair, for instance. God and plod have an appropriate anti-theological flavor, and Empson must have had fun rhyming Marx with sparks, remarks and larks. But the strongest effect here is the carefully achieved ease, the non-obtrusive quality of the rhyme scheme, and indeed of the poem's diction in general. And yet of course this discretion—the technical elements are there whether we consciously attend to them or not—is part of a design, and carries a modest freight of meaning, signaling the engagement of form even in a casual-seeming chat. This is not a style learned from despair, since the mood is so light. "I hope the gaiety of the thing comes through," Empson said later. "I felt I was in very good company" [CP 380]. But gaiety too needs style if it is to travel.

After the Japanese invasion of China in 1937, three universities (Peking National, Tsing Ha and Nankai) went into exile in Hunan province, and in November, they moved their Arts departments to the Heng Mountains. They stayed there, Empson among them, until February 1938. The "on" in his title refers to the slope of the mountain where his institute was situated.

"All in flight," Yeats says in the poem's epigraph, "and all / Deformed because there is no deformity / But saves us from a dream." "Saves" is Yeats's ironic imitation, through his character Michael Robartes, of our relief at not having to live up to our aspirations. Empson wants us not to be abashed by what he calls the poet's "scolding," and he relates "the holy mountain where I

live" to the quotation by mischievously invert-
ing its causal narrative. The mountain "straddles
two fates"—"personal immortality," Empson says
in a note, and "merging into a world soul"—but
here deformity does not shelter us from dreams,
it provokes dreaming. The mountain "has deformities to give / You dreams by all its paths and
gates" [CP 92].

But the poem is generally far more interested
in flight than in either deformities or dreams. The
first stanza suggests we all want to fly in some
mode or other. We are "eagles by hypothesis" and
"scorners eternal of the ground," yet no sooner
has Empson embarked on this metaphorical portrait than he abandons it for the comically literal
meaning of flight: he got here by plane—well, at
least when he didn't take a train or a bus. No high
aspirations here, just basic transportation. Then
he immediately shifts not into metaphor but into
double meaning: "It is true I flew, I fled."

And then there is—Empson never strays far
from the idea of flight in the poem—the local
drink which invites an escape from sobriety. "It is
not true," though, "That only an appalling fear /
Would drive a man to drink the stuff."

> Besides, you do not drink to steer
> Far out away into the blue.
>   The chaps use drink for getting near. [CP 93]

This is a little obscure in its apparent simplicity. The suggestion, I think, is that we don't drink in order to fly from company but to settle our nerves and improve the quality of the conversation. This was certainly Empson's own view of alcohol throughout his life, as Haffenden sympathetically shows.

Empson leaves the local scene for a general discussion of the current literary situation. His theme is still flight, of course. Isn't that what literature does? Run away from reality? Inhabit imagined worlds? Empson has a crisp and compact answer, which requires a little unfolding: "It struck me trying not to fly / Let them escape a bit too far" [CP 93]. The people objecting to flight—Empson probably has the critic F. R. Leavis and his followers in mind—are using their complaints about escapism as forms of escape, and are becoming literary stars in the process. What's missing in the objectors' argument is what it means to get "reality" into a poem and how much obliquity or compression is allowed.

> Indeed I finally agree
> > You do in practice have to say
> This crude talk about Escape
> > Cannot be theorized away. [CP 94]

Here is another reason for Empson's use of the Yeats quotation. For Yeats the dream was more real than what others call reality; a dream could be the one thing we are supposed to be loyal to, every defection from it a betrayal. Empson's question for fliers of all kinds is "what they fly from, whence they drop, / The truth that they forsake for show" [CP 94]. Whether the forsaken truth is a dream abandoned for mere reality, or a harsh reality abandoned for a safer dream, is a matter for individual poets and consciences. Empson sees that the "old word" will not do for the Modernist mentality, and that the poet's Dream, now capitalized, is a flop for everyone except the old poet. He goes on to complain in a friendly way about "the revolutionary romp" associated with Auden and Spender and other writers, and about the superrealism of Dylan Thomas, identified by transferred epithet as the creator of a "curly-headed toy." Empson then interrupts himself for a stanza to talk about bombs and actual airmen in the Japan–China War—he wants to keep these moral and literary metaphors within reach of literal uses—and returns to his argument about literary escape. I quote the next two stanzas in full.

Politics are what verse should
    Not fly from, or it all goes wrong.
I feel the force of that all right,
    And had I speeches they were song.

But really, does it do much good
    To put in verse however strong
The welter of a doubt at night
    At home, in which I too belong?
The heat-mists that my vision hood
    Shudder precisely with the throng.
England I think an eagle flight
    May come too late, may take too long.
What would I teach it? Where it could
    The place has answered like a gong.

What are these things I do not face,
    The reasons for entire despair,
Trenching the map into the lines
    That prove no building can be square?
Not nationalism nor yet race
    Poisons the mind, poisons the air,
Excuses, consequences, signs,
    But not the large thing that is there.
Real enough to keep a place
    Like this from owning its new heir;
But economics are divines,
    They have the floor, they have the flair. . . .
      [CP 95–96]

The last phrase is witty but feels like rather loose comment, perhaps provoked by the need to complete the count of lines for the stanza. For the rest, the two stanzas pursue a close and troubling argument concerning what a poet is supposed to do, and then more specifically, what Empson's own poetry can tell us about whatever it is that "poisons the mind, poisons the air." We are deep in the "sinister, confusing" atmosphere in which the storm is gathering.

"Had I speeches they were song": a transposition of Yeats's "True song, though speech," in the poem quoted in the epigraph. But does Empson have speeches; does he have more to say than what everyone else already thinks? This is a characteristically modest implied question—Empson was always modest when he was not distracted into arrogance—yet worth pondering. He doesn't exactly think like "the throng" but does feel he has nothing to teach his compatriots. He later thought "like a gong" was perhaps "rather too easy a sentiment," but the only snag with the phrase is the vagueness of its connection to "the place." He didn't mean all of "England" was sound: "The claim is that public opinion in England during this decade has been commonly right while independent of its political leaders and the machinery of propaganda" [CP 380]. The answer to his more than rhetorical question—"But really, does it do much good / To put in verse however strong / The welter of a doubt at night / At home, in which I too belong?"—is yes, but don't expect direct results.

And in fact Empson's next stanza is a fine example of hesitant speech turned into song. His argument finds itself, almost without a pause, thoroughly reversed. If his "entire despair" and the things he cannot face are not personal to him but part of a feeling that is international (if far from universal), then just saying what one can about this mood and these things will be the best any poem can do, and will refute all accusations of flight. At this point the poem represents a subtle and persuasive skepticism about history's apparent preoccupations. Nationalism and race are real enough of course, and they were everywhere in the 1930s, but they are, according to Empson, "excuses, consequences, signs" of something else:

> . . . the large thing that is there
> Real enough to keep a place
> Like this from owning its new heir.

This language seems vacant at first—"large thing," "real enough"—waiting for a meaning that hasn't arrived. And then we realize that the meaning is not going to arrive, can't get any nearer to us than such hints allow. We don't find the atmosphere "normal," but we don't find it anything else either. "Owning its new heir" is a bit mysterious, and Empson is probably thinking of whatever it is that keeps the Chinese from acknowledging more fully the groundswell of opposition to Chiang Kai-shek; the new heir would be the popular government not yet elected.

It's hard to act against a force that manifests itself only by excuses, consequences and signs, and Empson's next stanzas look at various refusals to act in the world at large: that of Communism generally and Stalin in particular; that of scholars who are prepared to wait forever for the right answer; that of people who sit at home and follow the news of violence abroad with informed delight. Empson doesn't claim to be acting importantly in these matters, only not to be "unpleasantly refined," and to be doing his job. The closest he comes to boasting is to say it is not "shameful to aver / A vague desire to be about / Where the important things occur . . ." [CP 96–97].

The poem seems to have settled the question of flight: evoked some of the many forms it can take, and marked a preference for some forms over others. But it ends with a renewed flicker of the wing:

I said I wouldn't fly again
    For quite a bit. I did not know.
Even in breathing tempest-tossed,
    Scattering to winnow and to sow,
With convolutions for a brain,
    Man moves, and we have got to go.
Claiming no heavy personal cost
    I feel the poem would be slow

Furtively finished on the plain.
    We have had the autumn here. But oh
That lovely balcony is lost
    Just as the mountains take the snow.
The soldiers will come here and train.
    The streams will chatter as they flow.
        [CP 97–98]

Flight now is not escape or aspiration but just movement: time, history, accident. Merely breathing lets us in for a storm. The poem ends on a double note of completed experience—"we have had the autumn"—and dispossession—"that lovely balcony is lost." The last lines give instances of what happens with or without Empson and his colleagues: snow comes to the mountains, the streams chatter, the soldiers arrive. The effect is hard to describe, but the place still feels particular even as the poem evokes its most general properties.

III

Empson's poem "Anecdote from Talk," first published in the volume *The Gathering Storm* in 1940, is the only work in *The Complete Poems* to provoke no comment at all from the eloquent and thoughtful editor John Haffenden. The Gardners are puzzled as to why Empson would want to tell the poem's story, and after saying the poem is "too wide of any conceivable literary mark to be parody, and too inconsistent and low-key in presentation to be memorable as poetry," they allow, in a flailing but appealing attempt not to be entirely unkind, that the poem "has a degree of rhythmic vigour and colloquial verisimilitude that is attractive" [Gardner 208].

The rhythms and the diction create the atmosphere of a popular ballad:

> John Watson was a tin-mine man
>> An expert of his kind.
> He worked up country in Malaya
>> On whisky, not resigned,
>> On whisky but not blind. [CP 89]

Watson tells a friend he feels "like death," and when the local manager of the company hears of Watson's mood he tells him to "beat it" (rhymes with "repeated"), because he'll be a "nuisance" if he dies at this station. Watson changes his mind—his feeling "like death" seems to have been an indication that he was thinking of killing himself—and says "I mean to live," but the manager still wants him to move on. "I'll keep no madman," he insists. Watson does move on, but his desire to live is not respected by the law of chance. The last stanza of the poem reads:

"This is the funny part," the manager says,
  "He was shot just the same.
Of course I had to pass him to a dickey job.

  Just the natives, no-one to blame.
  But it was quick how it came.
  Three weeks." [CP 89]

Empson's use of easy rhythms, and especially his ear for the Conradian manager's casual, unapologetic way of talking ("This is the funny part," "Of course," "Just the natives") at first masks the sadness of what is going on, and then enhances it. In the end the poem doesn't feel like a ballad at all, because it doesn't even feel like a poem. In this sense the Gardners are quite right, and even the vigor and verisimilitude are no help. It's as if the work falls from verse into prose, as if a prose destiny had been dogging it all along. A desolate, incomplete irony hangs in the air, and this must have been the effect Empson was after. The man who wanted to die does die, but only when he no longer wants to, and for no reason. There is no shape to the anecdote, it is merely a bad joke on the part of whoever writes the scripts of accident. Forget about learning a style from a despair, as Empson once suggested. It would be something to make the random look mildly less random for a moment.

Twelve years later—more perhaps, we don't seem to have a date for the writing of "Anecdote from Talk"—Empson published a ballad that doesn't die into something else. It was one of the last poems he wrote, followed only by "The Birth of Steel," the mock-Elizabethan masque he composed for the Queen of England's visit to Sheffield in 1954. The short poem was a translation of what Empson calls "a bit from a long ballad by Li Chi," written in 1945, and the basis of "a much praised opera." He couldn't do anything with the Chinese dialect in English, he said, but he found the right form for the sentiment. He reported on a later occasion that he "burst into tears when I found it just fell into international ballad metre" [CP 401].

The poem describes a meeting, perhaps the last, between two lovers. The man is about to return to the guerrilla war against the Japanese, and they stand together on a beach. The girl asks the man to make two models out of the mud around them, "yellow, deep, and thick": "one of me and one of you." He is then to mash them together, mixing them into a single paste. Next he will make two dolls again out of the mixture, creating a magical and enduring union:

"So shall your flesh be part of mine
   And part of mine be yours.
Brother and sister we shall be
   Whose unity endures.

"Always the sister doll will cry,
 Made in these careful ways,
Cry on and on, Come back to me,
 Come back in a few days." [CP 103]

If we suppose the man doesn't come back, that he dies in the war, this poem is even sadder than "Anecdote from Talk," but it is not desolate or defeated by chance. It does what ballads so often do: it shapes sorrow while in no way denying it. Empson thought the lyric represented "very fine metaphysical poetry at the end, when the clumsy little doll is to wait, through all eternity, just for a few days" [CP 401]. What makes "Anecdote from Talk" so bleak is the sense of how irremediably far from anything metaphysical it is. Nothing could be more different from the girl's touching and lyrical "few days" than the manager's mildly surprised and finally heartless "three weeks."

In a 1975 letter to Christopher Ricks, Empson explains that he took up writing again after the interruption created by his getting "absorbed in the war," but didn't return to poetry. The writing he has in mind is his essay on Buddhist sculpture, and pieces of his book *The Structure of Complex Words*. "There was a real gap, and an urgent practical need to get over it." He continues,

> but there was no such need to start writing poetry again, and the theme which all the modern

poets I admired had been working on, which I
had been working on too, had been blown out
like a candle. [CP 127]

The theme, as we have seen, was the mood and
mentality of waiting for the Second World War.

Empson concludes his letter with a mild recan-
tation of what he has just said, asserting that it is
"too glib, and some other process was probably at
work earlier to make the poetry I hammered out
strike me as unfit for publication" [CP 127–128].
The account is not at all glib, but it is mildly dis-
ingenuous. Empson of all people knows very well
that poets don't stop (or start) writing because a
theme awaits them or abandons them. What's intriguing is his identification of this theme, and his
sense that his poems were nothing without it.

The elegant swift movement of "Chinese Ballad," and Empson's own delight in the piece,
make clear that he didn't have to stop writing
poetry, but part of him thought he did, and the
blankness of "Anecdote from Talk," its metaphysical failure so to speak, feels like an enactment of
what may have been his reason. The work certainly illuminates Empson's explicit poetic fare-
well to verse.

This is called "Let it go," and was written "during the war," first published in the 1949 Collected
Poems.

It is this deep blankness is the real thing
        strange.
    The more things happen to you the more
        you can't
        Tell or remember even what they were.

    The contradictions cover such a range.
        The talk would talk and go so far aslant.
            You don't want madhouse and the whole
                thing there. [CP 99]

The poem plays in at least two different keys at once. The brevity, the rhythms and the rhymes (listening to Empson read this poem reminds us that he pronounced "were" the same as "wear") suggest discipline, a quick aphoristic disposal of a difficult business. A vagueness in the diction matches the mentioned blankness, and makes us feel we ought to know in advance what he is talking about: how to distinguish "the real thing" from others; how "things happen"; what "the whole thing there" is. The phrase "you don't want" may be the poet talking to himself, but he may be roping us in too: no sane person wants the kind of mental disaster he is simply calling "madhouse." In this curious usage it doesn't even seem to mean anything very literal ("you don't want to go mad, you wouldn't like to be locked away"), but rather a general chaos in us and the world around us: something like mayhem, only to do with the mind.

The main contrast in the poem though, the main contradiction perhaps, and what makes it such a strong instance of what Empson says he can't do anymore, is between the two stanzas. They seem to represent a sequence but they are saying different things, and thereby create the effect Empson uses so often in his poems where lines are both contrasted and repeated.

There is no story here about what causes the blankness, or even how it feels—except that it feels strange. There is an ambiguity in the claim about things happening. Are more of them happening than before, is that why you can't keep track? Or is it because you're losing track that it seems as if more are happening? "Tell or remember" is an interesting alternative, the "even" sounds a slightly peevish note, and "what they were" covers a huge amount of ground. Whatever they were, you don't know now.

But the contradictions seem to be something like the reverse of the blankness, a sort of retake of the idea of things happening to you more and more. You don't know what they are, you can't think coherently about them, yet you still know a contradiction when you see one, and they seem to be multiplying. The talk that would talk has a wonderful flavor of automatism to it, a sense of things getting completely out of control, but then "aslant" doesn't point to blankness, it points to the wrong path or the wrong angle.

The blankness is horrifying or disheartening then; the poet feels lost among the events around him, among his own failed responses to them. But there is worse. One could keep talking—or writing poems, say—without any sense of what sort of contradictions one was throwing up and throwing around, and this would be a disaster. It would be the equivalent of insanity and would entail everything that such a condition entails. There is a solution, however, a recourse to blankness in another mode: don't talk.

It's worth listening to the recording of Empson reading the poem, and not only to get an earful of the grandee English accent. It's the calmness that is most striking perhaps, a tone that seems almost offhand, as if this were not his poem, or as if he weren't there. The effect is of eminent sanity, and we can only agree with this voice. It knows what's strange and what isn't, and we certainly don't want anything to do with whatever it disapproves of. The talk, the madhouse, is a sort of mess on the floor. Best not noticed, or noticed only enough to avoid any future occurrences of this kind.

But then it seems as if we have to take the poem back from this voice. One of the ways of dealing with the real threat of "madhouse" would be to pretend the threat is not as real as all that. This would be a very Empsonian move, in accord with his definition of "the fundamental impulse of irony":

> to score off both the arguments that have been puzzling you, both sets of sympathies in your mind, both sorts of fool who will hear you; a plague on both their houses. It is because of the strength given by this antagonism that it seems to get so safely outside the situation it assumes, to decide so easily about the doubt which it in fact accepts. [SV 62]

The words to listen closely to here are "puzzling you," "sets of sympathies in your mind," and above all, "decide so easily about the doubt which it in fact accepts." This conversation may be entirely internal; the speaker or thinker gets to play the role of both fools; there are no others. These fools are pastoral figures in the theatre of our mind, simpletons delegated to disguise the complexity that besets us, turn it into a broad binary argument. This, I think, is what Empson's voice reading his poem may do, along with his seemingly so-casual diction: take one side in the quarrel, seem to decide easily about the doubt while allowing us to wonder how much doubt hides behind this apparent ease.

Empson spent his life perched among contradictions, they were his career in poetry and criticism. Had the talk not gone far aslant all along? Perhaps not. Perhaps he felt he had until now a way of seeing most contradictions as productive, as a form of liberty, as something people could make up their own minds about, and never the end of the tale. In *Some Versions* he lists various possibilities for the function of "a good irony": "to reconcile the opposites into a larger unity, or suggest a balanced position by setting out two extreme views, or accept a lie (more or less consciously) to find energy to accept a truth, or something like that" [SV 63]. This is a complicated scenario but it ends in poise and/or action. The blankness identified in the poem is the state of seeing the contradictions and no longer knowing what to do with them, except to register the mess. What would happen if unity, balance, and a creative relation between lies and truth all felt like unusable old fictions, so far aslant?

SIX

Sibylline Leaves

"The mind is complex and ill-connected like an audience."

William Empson, *Some Versions of Pastoral*

I

Empson's practical answer to the question with which I ended my last chapter was that if poetry becomes just talk, we should talk about it—in prose. He had been working on *The Structure of Complex Words* since 1936—some of the thinking for the book went back as far as 1932—and, as we have seen, he was keen to get back to it after the war. In 1939, before returning to England, he had written to a friend, "I wish to God I could get on with my mad little literary book, the Sibylline leaves are gradually being thrown away by the servant" [Haffenden I 528–529]. The word "mad" is just a self-deprecating joke here, and doesn't take us anywhere near the hospital, but it is interesting that it crops up. It would be too schematic to say that Empson continued to write mad books in prose to keep himself from the more extreme madness of poetry, yet something had changed.

143

Empson's later criticism still straddles convictions and uncertainties with tremendous energy and wit, but he is on the whole, as he was not before, doing what he can to resolve matters rather than complicate them. He says, for example, that metaphor is a "very baffling topic" and "perhaps too fundamental to be cleared up," but also thinks it would make a "valuable" object of study "if one knew how to set about it" [CW 184, 175]. We might think his confession that he finds it "hard to choose between theories at all in this field except by coming across examples in which one theory works better than another" registers a sound scientific position. Empson regards (or pretends to regard) his difficulty as a sign of "a lack of intellectual grasp" [CW 368].

He makes a distinction among the readers he imagines for *The Structure of Complex Words.* "The reader interested in literary criticism," he says, "will find his meat only in a central area," namely the chapters on the uses of particular words in Pope, Milton, Erasmus, Shakespeare, Austen and Wordsworth. This reader "need not bother" with the seven theoretical chapters, and Empson "will not be depressed" if the same reader ignores the three appendices, "which are merely rather amateur attempts to push some problems from Philosophy out of the way." He will however feel that he has failed if the literary reader does not return from the critical chapters to the first two, "Feelings in Words" and "Statements in Words," because "the conclusions drawn from them are worth looking into" [CW 1].

Needless to say, most of us who read this book read it straight through, and if it feels a little unprofessional even for literary study, let alone philosophy and linguistics, we may remember R. P. Blackmur's definition of criticism as "the formal discourse of an amateur." Cleanth Brooks's identification of the author of *The Structure of Complex Words* as "the incorrigible amateur, the man with a knack" perhaps goes a little too far in this direction. Empson himself says he is trying to keep away from what he calls "intellectual buzzsaws," but then offers two remarkable qualifications of his attempt. First, he says he can't avoid these questions unless he knows where they are. And second, he says this answer is false anyway, "because I think that even a moderate step forward in our understanding of language would do a great deal to improve literary criticism, and in any case to improve our general reading capacity" [CW 1].

A recurring powerful thought is that dictionaries, perhaps necessarily, list different meanings of words as . . . different meanings. Not only do they often fail to distinguish between principal and subsidiary meanings, they must by their vocation neglect to say that the different meanings of a word are likely to haunt any of its particular uses. I would like to say that this haunting always takes place, but Empson doesn't usually go that far. He does say that a word may have a "'connotation' or feeling which is faintly present in all its uses" [CW 406], and he is certainly interested in "the interactions of the senses of a word" [CW 391], because this is what his book is about.

Throughout the work Empson fails creatively to make an important distinction: between meanings that are in some way in the words, implicit or explicit in their ordinary use, and meanings created by particular applications of the words: "being 'in' the word is of course a matter of degree" [CW 25]. I say "fails creatively" because although we can and sometimes must make these distinctions, their theoretical interest lies in the chance of keeping possibilities open— and all the more so because the possibilities are real and practical, just not always in play at the same time.

Empson's emphasis is constantly on the "rich obscure practical knowledge" [CW 438] that any language holds in trust for us, and this emphasis allows him to pursue individual cases, and to refuse definitions that would keep him away from the active life of the language he wants to explore.

"The connection between theory and practice, where both are living and growing, need not be very tidy" [CW 434]. Empson is especially interested in what he calls the emotive or slangy use of certain words, suggesting that a person is likely to make up his or her mind "in a practical question of human relations, much more in terms of these vague rich intimate words than in the clear words of [his or her] official language" [CW 158]. The recurrence of the word "rich" is important, and we have seen it at work in an earlier chapter. It names something like generosity in words, and the chance of generosity in the user of them. Richness in *Some Versions of Pastoral* is glossed as "readiness for argument not pursued" [SV 145].

"Such words give us an insight into the thought of a given period," Empson says, and may also "form a kind of shrubbery of smaller ideas," which helps us to defend ourselves against our own big ideas.

There is a main puzzle for the linguist about how much is "in" a word and how much in the general purpose of those who use it, but it is this shrubbery, a social and not very conscious matter, sometimes in conflict with organized opinion, that one would expect to find only able to survive because somehow inherent in their words. This may be an important matter

for a society, because its accepted official beliefs may be things that would be fatal unless
in some degree kept at bay. [CW 158]

Empson is thinking of the "official beliefs" of
Christianity and Buddhism, but we can call up
plenty of other "official" assumptions that will
work only if we accept them less than whole-
heartedly, and his picture of society is both complex and appealing. Greeks and Elizabethans
held Greek and Elizabethan worldviews. They
also, because they were human beings with lives
to live, dissented from these views on all kinds
of occasions. Empson says something similar of
Dr. Johnson: "probably the parts of his thought
which are by this time most seriously and rightly
admired were not carried on his official verbal
machinery but on colloquial phrases." I add only
that it is not just the words in the shrubbery that
do the counter-official work. The official words
will do it too, if they are given the right ironic or
speculative inflection.

"A poet is not building an intellectual system,"
Empson writes, "he is recording a time when
his mind was trying out an application of the
thoughts, not proving a doctrine about them"
[CW 6–7]. Recording a time is a fine, precise
thought. Empson wants us to see that the cri-
terion of truth has its place even in imaginary

conditions, whether to do with poetry or with our responses to other people: "The point is not that their truth or falsity is irrelevant, but that you are asked to imagine a state of mind in which they would appear to be true" [CW 12]. This is his solution to a very old problem concerning "beliefs" in literature: "not that we separate them from their consequences but that we imagine some other person who holds them, an author or a character, and thus get a kind of experience of what their consequences (for a given sort of person) really are" [CW 9]. "I do not see," he says, in a grand refusal to acknowledge what is so difficult for everyone else, "that the subtlety of the process detaches it from any connection with fact" [CW 14].

Truth, consequences, fact: all imaginary perhaps but all imaginable, discussable. Empson is saying that even poetry full of feeling is structured by thought, does not consist of mere mood or imagery, and he is inclined to believe that feeling without thought, if not a literal impossibility, will not find its way into language. The unofficial doctrines have at least as large a place in our lives as the official ones. There is such a thing, Empson says, as "the logic of . . . unnoticed propositions" [CW 39].

This sense of the life of words—"it seems to me very likely that there is an inner grammar of complex words like the overt grammar of sentences" [CW 253]—is both intensely practical and largely mythical. Practical because we experience it every day, and because Empson has such brilliant things to say about particular examples. And mythical because it all takes place in a location we can neither ignore nor inspect. In *The Structure of Complex Words* Empson calls it "the background of the mind" [CW2, 69], "the subconsciousness" [CW 10], and "the back of the mind" [CW 57, 120, 200, 203, 426], a phrase he likes to use elsewhere too [SV 27, 103, 176]. Sometimes the notion of being in the back is enough: "at the back of the metaphor," "at the back of an ironical joke" [SV 33, 55]. It is a spot where words and meanings "hang about" [CW 274], where ideas are "not so often believed as feared to be possible" [CW 168], where different, even opposed meanings congregate without quarrelling. It is where Pope's distinct uses of the word "wit" in *The Essay on Criticism* stay together, where his jokes and his seriousness are never out of touch with each other.

It is also where most readers or viewers will find, if they find it at all, their reaction to Fortinbras's terrible gag about Hamlet.

Let four captains
Bear Hamlet, like a soldier, to the stage;

For he was likely, had he been put on,
To have proved most royally.

The obvious, decorous meaning is that Hamlet would have done well in war and governance, if he had had the chance, but the pileup of "like," the stage, and "put on" suggests the new leader has wandered into a swamp of dramatic or Freudian irony. Now the implication is that Hamlet has always been an actor, never offstage even in his most intimate moments, and that even death is not going to change him. Empson thinks this is a mistake on the writer's part—although of course Shakespeare doesn't have the "appalling persistence" of Joyce when it comes to puns [CW 66].

But Empson is mainly describing, not judging, and he thinks the Freudian slip can even serve common sense: "when a man is dutifully deceiving himself he will often admit the truth in his metaphors" [CW 338]. The back of the mind here looks like the depths of the mind. Still, this perspective is also part of Empson's plan. Complex words really are complex, either in themselves or in the uses to which they are put, and all we can do, if we wish to understand their working, is track the examples we meet to whatever parts of the mind they light up for us, and whatever regions of the "socially complicated" world [CW 28].

II

The chapter on *King Lear* in *The Structure of Complex Words* is one of the masterpieces of literary criticism of any time, and leaves us thrilled and exhausted in ways that resemble the effects of the play itself. Empson would think this comparison far too grandiose, and I am not suggesting that his writing imitates or competes with Shakespeare's, only that it fully rises to the challenge of an extraordinary reading, and that here as elsewhere in his work, the style of the criticism performs as well as declares an interpretation.

In *King Lear* we have a "group of ideas" that cluster round words like fool, madman, jester, clown, simpleton; and somewhere among them is the figure of the "ordinary simple man, who is held to be somehow right about life though more pretentious figures fail to see it" [CW 105]. The most famous exposition of this trope is Erasmus's *The Praise of Folly*, and Empson devotes a preliminary chapter to exploring the set of meanings collected and set in motion there. Erasmus (and the Middle Ages before him) was a little too religious for Empson, who says he "cannot see . . . that Shakespeare makes any serious use of the idea that God will forgive us because we are all fools, which was the crown of the structure of medieval fool-theory" [CW 107]. Erasmus certainly believed in this idea, but his text suggests rather that we are not fools enough, that true folly is beyond us, and a secular version of this thought is precisely what animates some of the most magnificent moments of Shakespeare's play.

In Erasmus Folly herself sings the praise of folly, and of course does it foolishly. She is not joking when she says the most foolish thing anyone has ever done is die to save others, especially if like Jesus Christ you are dying to save a whole hopeless species. Erasmus's irony is circular and complete, it invites all kinds of thoughts, some easy and some difficult, but we can't tip it into any kind of sermonizing. Whatever steps we take in that direction will look ridiculous.

Shakespeare's version of folly is secular, and reads now as if he were entirely up to date with our twenty-first-century assumptions about rational choice, self-making and self-seeking. A good instance, as we saw in the last chapter, occurs in the conversation between the formal fool, the king's jester, and the accidental one that the Earl of Kent has become. Neither man is going to abandon the king to the literal and metaphorical storm that is approaching. The fool will stay, and the other fool will stay too: loyalty in this context can only appear as a failure to be wise.

The storm's other name is madness, and Kent and the Fool are going to meet up with the Earl of

Gloucester's son Edgar, who is pretending to be a lunatic, that is, neither a jester nor an unprofessional simpleton but still part of the folly family. At this point four fools are materially represented by particular characters—a clown, a man who goes mad, a man who pretends to be mad, and a man who is stupidly, even insanely loyal—and several other meanings of the word float about in the language of the play. The other chief sense of "mad" is within reach here too. When Lear feels himself to be in danger of weeping rather than raging, he says "I shall go mad." He will go mad because he can't get mad, can't find a sane form for his anger.

I'm sure Empson is right to place Shakespeare at some distance from Erasmus, in spite of the close echo. Erasmus has the folly of Christ as his model, and the further Socratic folly of over-intelligent humans who imagine they are wise. Shakespeare has the wisdom of the wise as his target. This is not false worldly wisdom, as in the religious view, it is the real, depressing, all too frequent thing, as we have seen in Empson's reading of Sonnet 94. Shakespeare is reflecting, through his characters, on the sheer good sense of leaving others to the storm if you can get out of it. We can't, alas, say such behavior is wrong because we are quite likely to do the same ourselves. But we can celebrate those who are crazy enough or noble enough to do otherwise.

The Fool's position is quite particular. It's his job to be funny, and Empson is right to remind us of "the malice which is part of his role." We don't have to think of him as "high-minded and self-sacrificing" [CW 133]. But he does stay rather than run, and surely Empson is wrong to say "the Fool understands about madness because he is mad himself" [CW 133]. He imitates folly in all kinds of ways, but no one in the play seems further from insanity. When he says he would rather be anything than a fool—Lear has just threatened to have him whipped—he corrects himself instantly with a thought we may find sorrowful or sympathetic or merely realistic. "I had rather be any kind o' thing than a fool: and yet I would not be thee, nuncle."

"The very subtle thought of *Lear* was inherent in the language," Empson claims, and specifically in the play of meanings hovering around the idea of the fool [CW 115]. This inherence means that even the mild verb "reflecting" as I used it above is probably too strong and too intentional—not for Empson, but for me. Shakespeare had only to strike certain notes, and a crowd of implications and associations would start the rich but perhaps ultimately unmanageable interpretative work in the audience's mind. His mastery was in the timing and temper of the notes.

"The subject of *Lear* is renunciation," Empson quotes George Orwell as saying. "The idea of renunciation is examined in the light of the complex idea of folly," and this is the thread he follows throughout his chapter [CW 125]. What's initially wrong with Lear's renunciation of power and authority, the division of his kingdom among his three daughters, or as it happens between two of them, is the elaborate pretense he has set up for his abdication. Empson remarks on "the speed and violence" that Shakespeare lends to this "scene like a fairy-story" [CW 126].

Lear asks his daughters, "Which of you shall we say doth love us most?" He is not asking how much they love him, but what they will say, wondering how he will judge the competition in rhetoric. Two of his daughters, the ugly sisters of this linguistic fairy tale, read the invitation correctly, amply producing ghastly versions of the verbal show required. The other refuses to take part in the charade, and again Shakespeare point us towards a question of utterance rather than feeling, as if he has been working on speech act theory. "What can you say," Lear asks Cordelia, "to draw / A third more opulent than your sisters? Speak." She says nothing. No, she says "Nothing," but of course the spoken word is not nothing, in this situation it is a disastrous assertion. Her father tells her that "nothing will come of nothing."

This is not the place for a long exploration of the theme, but it seems to be the case with all the many uses of the word "nothing" in the play—referring to a speech, a letter, a piece of nonsense, a lack of identity—that the operative meaning constantly lies with the opposite term: saying something; reading something; meaning something; being something.

Later in the play Lear repeats his apparently pragmatic formula with a slightly different wording: "nothing can be made of nothing." It's worth pausing over the awful trick that language and his own vanity are playing on the king. It is mathematically true that if you add nothing to nothing you have nothing, but the maxim is ruined if your nothing hides an unmistakable something.

We have quickly come a long way from the initial game. The false saying of love by two daughters has become the true saying of dismissal and degradation. The true if slightly prickly saying of love by the other daughter has become an absence. The question now is not what anybody says, but what a king is when he is not a king, and more generally, what anyone is when they step out or fall out of a social role that has a recognized name and status.

Empson goes much further than this question of lost or baffled identity, though. If he writes so forcefully in his later work about how wrong religion, and especially Christianity, can be, here he offers what may be the best defense of superstition ever invented. Commenting on critical responses to Cordelia's death and various attempts to rescue the dignity of the gods who seem to act only as a disguise for chance, he suggests that grand ironies in Hardy's style are just as bad as pious attempts at uplift. "To believe in a spirit who only jeers at you is superstitious without having any of the advantages of superstition. . . . If this is the atheist view of tragedy it is as disagreeable as the Christian view" [CW 154].

What are the advantages of superstition? Very briefly, if it is put to imaginative and ambitious use, it will allow us to think about chance, character, and whatever order the world is supposed to have without recourse to religion or fatalism. It will allow us to see tragedy where other perspectives will show us only bad luck or bad habits, and we can evoke it, if we inhabit the pre-Christian world of King Lear, by Greek names or anonymous terms like "the heavens," and of course by the recurring word Nature.

Empson begins to unpack this set of evocations by suggesting that Lear's early address to the "dear goddess" Nature offers "room for a superstitious idea that his curses really affect Nature and bring bad luck all round" [CW 130]. We know this idea is superstitious because we know Nature doesn't care what we say, yet we also know that magic and metaphor have truths to tell us about the world. At the end of his magnificent speech about need, Lear appeals to the heavens, begging them that they will "fool me not so much / To take it tamely," a speech that Empson says "touches off the storm." Really? Is that how it works? Empson's answer is exemplary:

> At least there seems no doubt that it would be so taken by the audience, who were accustomed to melodramas in which thunder comes as an immediate reply. The storm in Nature is no doubt partly the image of Lear's mind, but it is also an attack upon him, whether from the stern justice of God or the active malice of the beings he has prayed to. The use of the term *fool* acts as a strong support for the theory of malice. . . . Every time Lear prays to the gods, or anyone else prays on his behalf, there are bad effects immediately. [CW 134]

The hesitation about the source of the attack—God or the gods—represents different views in the imagined audience, but the imagery will work whatever our theology is, as long as we are not using it to shut out our fears. The ideas of justice and even malice, on this scale, take us well beyond being jeered at. This sort of response to prayer suggests a much larger story about human helplessness. Empson goes on to propose that another famous speech of Lear's ("Take physic, pomp") invites us to think that "Nature does you good, but only when in its more appalling forms" [CW 137].

Whether Nature does us good or not, it is what there is, and in this play there is no other agency to which we can put our questions. "Is there any cause in nature that makes these hard hearts?" Lear asks, in what Empson calls "his clearest expression of the feeling of mystery in the evil of the world." There is no shortage of opinions about nature and providence in the play—almost every character offers at least one—but "it does not appear," Empson says, "that any of the views are made to seem adequate to the mystery of the world as it is presented" [CW 144].

This surely is the ultimate advantage of superstition. It does not claim knowledge it doesn't have, and it does not deny its bafflement. On the contrary, it dramatizes its disarray. You ask the gods not to do something, and they do it at once. Religion in its consolatory, schematizing sense is always akin to paranoia, and paranoia is often close to being right—about the extent of our need for a lurid story if nothing else. Which do we prefer? That the world's horrors occur by chance or by maleficent design? Which view will make us feel better if "the world is a place in which good intentions get painfully and farcically twisted by one's own character and by unexpected events" [CW 154–155]?

When Gloucester says the gods "kill us for their sport," he is not articulating "a solid doctrine," as Empson puts it, but he is connecting his thought to "the fundamental imagery of the play" [CW 141]. Edgar's response—

How should this be?
Bad is the trade that must play fool to sorrow,
Angering itself and others.

—refers to his own role in deceiving and protecting his father, but also, Empson adds, "helps us to define the gods":

The clash of these two great sentences makes us see them as creatures cruel and senseless through their own suffering, the contempt of whose irony unites them to what they mock. [CW 142]

I'm not sure Edgar's line quite makes this contribution, but this is just the effect of the play at large. This vision of the gods as cruel creatures implies a whole tortured universe. Empson associates the image with "the root idea of tragedy that the sacrifice of the hero re-unites his tribe with Nature or with supernatural forces" [CW 142], and it is in this sense that Lear can become "the scapegoat who has collected all this wisdom for us . . . viewed at the end with a sort of hushed envy, not I think really because he has become wise but because the general human desire for experience has been so glutted in him; he has been through everything" [CW 157].

The Greek gods in the play (and Nature and the heavens) are not just decorative, or stand-ins for whatever deities pagan Britain had, they are precise equivalents for what they were in Aeschylus or Sophocles: sources of any order or clemency there is in the world, but also of all its chaos and cruelty. We would blame them if we could; as it is, we worship them and fear them and hope for the best.

> Lear has made a fool of himself on the most cosmic and appalling scale possible: he has got on the wrong side of the next world as well as on the wrong side of this one. I do not think one need extract any more theology from the gods. [CW 155]

Empson's "not I think really because he has become wise" is not a denial of Lear's wisdom, only of its relevance. This seems to me a remarkably subtle point. Lear has learned a real lesson, "not merely through suffering, but through having been a clown." But then "this mood of greatness arises in him as a sort of wild flower, almost unconnected with anything else. The play does not allow him to keep it" [CW 146–147]. Perhaps one can't keep it and live. The paradox of being right about the mystery of this world and the next by getting on the wrong side of both is almost too deep to contemplate. "Being right" here seems to mean arriving at a story less deluded than most, but only available in some sort of delusion.

"Ambiguous gifts, as what gods give must be"—we have read the line in "This Last Pain" [CP 53]. The repeated letter "g" creates a kind of stutter, as if the poem were ambiguous about ambiguity. And indeed, what could be ambiguous about the terrible gifts showered on the unfortunate humans in *King Lear*? Cruelty, deceit, poverty, madness, death and bereavement are just the chief among the unkind donations. But then what if they are the price of even a useless wisdom, the discovery of your daughter's love, and an entirely new sympathy for the wretched of the earth? The idea of a price troubles the notion of the gift, of course, yet since both price and gift are metaphors for a relation we can't name otherwise, we may feel that even among unequivocal horrors we have not quite done with ambiguity. We can certainly decide the price of wisdom is too high, and if Lear and Cordelia were historical persons most of us would emphatically do so, and want other lives for them. But since they are characters in perhaps the fiercest and most imaginative portrayal we have of the intractable world that is ours, we can hardly wish for them anything other than just the lives and deaths they have.

III

I want to glance at one more of Empson's complex words, because he thinks it functions very differently from "fool" and its relatives, and because it will show something of the range of his inquiries. It also displays a certain recurrence and consistency, since his main example is still Shakespeare, and the questions raised in *King Lear* have not gone away, only found another, rather shabbier home. The word is "honest" and the Shakespeare play in question is *Othello*.

The word has the familiar meanings of "truthful" or "to be trusted," and a lot of now obsolete or rare connections with the word "honor." Used of a woman it means "chaste" or even "virginal"; used of a servant or anyone perceived to be of lower station than oneself, it has a note of cheerful condescension. A phrase like "to be honest" can mean anything from "I'm going to tell you the truth, although it may not be a good idea" to "I'm so glad to have something nasty to say to you." The *Oxford English Dictionary*, not notable for its jokes, must at least be smiling when it glosses the phrase "honest John" as "a truthful, trustworthy, or sincere man; a type of surface-to-surface ballistic missile designed to carry a nuclear warhead." It does say the second meaning is "now historical."

Empson's great aim, his implausible task, is to discover how the infinitely deceitful Iago, so often called honest and himself so skillful a manipulator of the term, could actually in some sense be honest—deceiving others, for example, because he is himself so undeceived. Empson likes to repeat the idiom "blow the gaff" in this context. The words "honest" and "honesty" are used 52 times in Othello, Empson tells us. *King Lear* uses the word "fool" "nearly as often"—47 times, Empson notes elsewhere—"but does not treat it as a puzzle, only as a source of profound metaphors." "There is no other play in which Shakespeare worries a word like that" [CW 218]. The slightly archaic use of "worry" as a transitive verb is very effective. The only ordinary context I can think of for this idiom is when a dog worries a piece of cloth or a toy or a newspaper. What's more, Shakespeare "hated" the word "honest,"

Empson says. Or more precisely, there was something he hated "in the word": "a peculiar use, at once hearty and individualist, which was then common among raffish low people but did not become upper-class till the Restoration" [CW 218]. "The word was in the middle of a rather complicated process of change." It

> came to have in it a covert assertion that the man who accepts the natural desires, who does not live by principle, will be fit for such warm uses of honest as imply "generous" and "faithful to friends," and to believe this is to disbelieve the Fall of Man. [CW 218]

Empson is moving very fast here, and I don't think he means Shakespeare hates these implications, only the fact that it seems to be impossible for his characters to use the word in this sense without a patronizing effect. The Concordance shows, Empson says, that Shakespeare "never once allows the word a simply hearty use between equals" [CW 218]. So we might think that "the way everybody calls Iago honest amounts to a criticism of the word itself" [CW 219]. And no doubt, a criticism of those who habitually use it in this way, normalizing double-talk. There are plenty of "honest" people, that is, who are crooked in all kinds of other ways. But Empson thinks this good sense, honest itself in a fashion, doesn't get us anywhere near the complications of Iago's character. A sort of honesty in Iago is dramatically more interesting than a pride in his own villainy, which is more usually attributed to him.

Nineteenth-century critics, Empson says, saw Iago as an abstraction, a representation of evil, and plenty of later critics have followed the tradition. In a marvelous reversal of usual priorities, Empson asks us to prefer a single word to a package of important meanings. Writers and critics have often evoked fancies and daydreams of evil, he says, but with a vagueness that almost robs the term of meaning. "Iago may not be a 'personality,' but he is better than these; he is the product of a more actual interest in a word" [CW 231]. "The puns on *honest* take the stage," Empson says [CW 238].

How does this work, though? When Othello tells Iago's wife, Emilia, that it is from her husband that he has learned of Desdemona's (supposed) infidelity, she is taken aback, and repeats the idea in astonishment: "My husband!" "My husband say that she was false?" Othello insists:

I say thy husband: dost understand the word?
My friend, thy husband, honest, honest Iago.

As Empson says, "Othello means no irony against Iago, and it is hard to invent a reason for his repetition of *honest*" [CW 226]. But if "honest" has among its implications, to summarize rapidly what I am taking from Empson, "alert to, even disgusted by the deceptions of the world, including one's own murky games," then we can see Othello as desperately caught between the patronizing and the unmasking sense of the word: Iago is a jolly good fellow and perhaps the only person who sees the dark truth of things. This would be why Empson calls the line "appalling," as he evokes "the hearty use and the horror of it" [CW 227].

We can also think—we could think forever—about the intricate conversation between Iago and Othello, where the servant accuses the master of making honesty a vice, because that is what happens when one is stupidly honest.

> *Iago.* To be direct and honest is not safe.
>   I thank you for this profit, and from hence
>   I'll love no friend, sith love breeds such
>   offence
> *Othello.* Nay stay; thou should'st be honest.
> *Iago.* I should be wise; for honesty's a fool,
>   And loses that it works for.
> *Othello.*   By the world,
>   I think my wife be honest, and think she
>   is not.

What is striking is the way honesty gets entangled with folly here, and with uncertainty, as if we had returned to the moral universe of *King Lear*. And in a way we have. The twist, though, and one that does suggest Shakespeare is worrying a word rather than playing with it, is that honesty cancels itself out in such excessive maneuvers: it's just honest to see how foolish honesty is. Wisdom is better than honesty because wisdom knows the score. But then you have to be "really" honest to acknowledge this wisdom. The thought is circular and repellent, yet hard to steer entirely clear of in any fully socialized world. Perhaps Iago's real vice is his determination not to be a fool.

We should note too that this rampant cynicism, in *Othello*, is using the language of Puritan morality, and at one point Empson makes the brilliant suggestion that Iago himself "is a satire on the holy thought of Polonius: 'To thine own self be true . . . thou canst not then be false to any man'" [CW 231]. What if the self I want to be true to is that of a cruel depressive who loves sowing havoc in the world not because he is evil but because it's fun—or it's the closest thing to fun to that he can manage?

I don't think *Othello* is more disturbing than *King Lear*, but it is more intimately involved with the ways we talk to ourselves and others, and in this sense Empson's chapter is about meanings that are very close to a word, and not the vast

realms of implication a word may conjure up.
Here the realms are the reverse of vast; petty and
demeaning rather. But we do see what happens
when puns take the stage, and language is recognized as the consummate performance artist
that it is.

SEVEN

The Smoke of Hell

> "The net effect of this language system was not
> to keep these people ignorant of what they were
> doing, but to prevent them from equating it with
> their old, 'normal' knowledge of murder and lies."
>
> Hannah Arendt, *Eichmann in Jerusalem*

I

In 1952, a year after the publication of *The Structure of Complex Words*, Empson returned to
England from China. A year later, he became
Professor of English at the University of Sheffield, where he taught until he retired in 1971.
He lived part of the time in Sheffield, cheerfully
enjoying, in Seamus Perry's words, "the agree-
able squalor that was his preferred mode of existence," and part of the time in London where
he and his wife Hetta presided—perhaps not the
right word—over the changing population of a
Bohemian community that lived in their house.

The criticism Empson wrote after his return
to England did not only seek to resolve matters
rather than complicate them, as I have suggested
about the work of his middle years. It was largely,

as Christopher Norris says, a series of attempts at rescue [Norris 35]. Empson's major work of this period, *Milton's God* (1961), sought to save the poem from the Christians by proving that Milton, far from delivering on his promise to "justify the ways of God to men," had honorably failed to defend the ways of a vicious and tyrannical monster. His work on Coleridge, both in a long essay and in his introduction to *Coleridge's Verse* (1972), a volume he edited with David Pirie, went even further: the idea was to rescue Coleridge from Coleridge, the younger poet from the older man listening to nothing but his Christian superego. And the book he was working on before he died, *Faustus and the Censor* (published in 1987), resurrected a version of Marlowe's play that two well-known print versions had managed to bury.

"The belief in progress may sometimes be delusory," Empson writes in *Milton's God,* but he offers an impressive instance where the belief is entirely justified. Around 600–500 BCE, he says, the great religions of China, India and the Mediterranean Basin gave up human sacrifice. "The effect of this . . . was to make them conceive a God of all mankind, transcendent and metaphysically one with Goodness; though both India and China tended to conceive an Absolute rather than a Person" [MG 241]. The point of Empson's excursion into comparative religion is to show that his attack on Christianity is not an attack on faith, and that Christianity is not just one more among what he had earlier called "the creeds of the world" [CP 55].

> Among the various universal religions which were formed as a result of this change and still survive, Christianity is the only one which ratted on the progress, the only one which dragged back the Neolithic craving for human sacrifice into its basic structure. [MG 241]

Empson is not attacking the idea of sacrifice either: "I agree at once that no good mode of life is secure unless its participants are prepared to make sacrifices for it." Even the Neolithic chieftain who sacrificed his son "was assumed to be giving up what was most valuable to him, very unwillingly, for the good of his people." "The moral interest is in the sacrificer and the sacrificed, not in the deity who is gratified" [MG 243]. The double focus of his complaint is clear and intimately troubling: human sacrifice should not be part of anyone's worship, and it is disastrous that we have learned to think this is not what is happening in the case of Jesus Christ's death. A greedy god wanted him dead, even though (or because) he was his son.

The whole of *Milton's God* rests on these ideas: the horrible god and our failure to see the horror.

In the particular instance where he speaks of progress and makes the comparison, Empson's target is the doctrine of the Trinity when it is offered as an excuse. "The Father is in some sense identical with the Son, therefore the story means that God mysteriously sacrificed himself on behalf of mankind; because he so loved the world" [MG 243]. Empson's "in some sense" and "mysteriously" give his game away; he is not going to allow this doctrine even a neutral description. He is willing to believe that the doctrine "was of crucial importance in shoring up the structure enough to make intelligent men with good feelings trust it" [MG 243], but intelligent men with good feelings can be wrong, and in this case their trust prevents them from seeing the Orwellian double-talk of the doctrine. And more broadly the double-talk allows Christians to pick whichever aspect of the deity they want. This is how modest monks become torturers when they gain power, and Empson generalizes this "mental trick" [MG 244] to include modern professions like medicine: the established doctor respects all the taboos he used to criticize when he was a medical student. Empson's interest is not just in our performing the trick, or persuading us not to, but in how the trick works.

This is exactly the method of his criticism all along, although earlier it was used to reveal riches of meaning and now it unmasks our self-deceit. And in the generous mode we have met so often, he is ready to regard the trick as in itself perfectly ordinary, part of our equipment for surviving difficult times and questions.

> Our minds have a wonderful readiness to satisfy themselves with admittedly false identities, but any orderly schooling needs to drive the process into the background of its area of practical work. . . . Regarded simply as a bit of mental equipment, [the trick] carries within itself a kind of recognition that the matter would bear looking into, or an impulse to do that later, though enough is settled for an immediate decision. Thus we should make terms with the process rather than struggle to renounce it. [MG 244–245]

Should we make terms with the process? Well, we have to if we can't renounce it. But we can—and this is Empson's essential and very useful point—recognize misuses of it. We should realize (yet all too often don't) that the story of a loving god who likes to torture his son is not a metaphysical mystery but a moral atrocity; a means, Empson says, "by which Christians hide from themselves the insane wickedness of their God" [MG 245]. "The Creed of St Athanasius . . . amounts to saying that the Father and the Son both are and are not identical, and that you will go to Hell unless you believe both" [MG 246]. It's not believing both of two contradictory things that is the snag. That's a logical rule that sometimes has to be broken. It's believing both of *these* two things, and hiding from the consequences—without even knowing you're hiding.

Milton's God is certainly governed by what Norris calls Empson's "ruling obsession" [Norris 35]—John Haffenden puts the whole of the second half of Empson's life under the sign of Against the Christians. And there are times when Empson's lashing out against God makes you think he is running some kind of political campaign against a live enemy. God is "monstrously wicked," motivated by "infinite malice." The rebelling angels are right in their "passionate loathing" of him. "What Christians are worshipping . . . is literally the Devil." In a heartier mood Empson makes a detailed dictator comparison: "The picture of God in the poem . . . is astonishingly like Uncle Joe Stalin; the same patience under an appearance of roughness, the same flashes of joviality, the same thorough unscrupulousness, the same real bad temper" [MG 10, 38, 24, 260, 146]. These swipes are delivered with such relish and righteousness that it is hard to remember that this God is not human. And even harder to remember that God is not even the chief target of

Empson's assaults. The chief targets are the inventors of this God, the people who opted out of the moral progress that was taking place in 600–500 BCE, and everyone since who has failed to see the horror of the invention. "The Christian God the Father . . . is the wickedest thing yet invented by the black heart of man" [MG 251].

I'm not sure I quite believe this, and wouldn't know how to run the quantitative comparison anyway. But certainly Empson was on to something; still is. In 1975 I wrote a piece on him in the *New York Review of Books*, full of praise for his writing but mildly patronizing, I'm afraid, about his passion for flogging what I then thought was a dead theological horse. I suggested that his "principal literary enemies (C. S. Lewis, E.M.W. Tillyard, and God) are all dead," and professed surprise not at his view of Christianity but at "his strained insistence that we have to have a view of Christianity." Like many other people in 1975, I thought Christianity was a thing of the past, and we had other worries. I don't need to say how wrong I was.

For some time I didn't know Empson had responded to this piece, because he didn't send his letter to the journal. John Haffenden kindly showed me the draft in 1987 (and later printed it in his edition of the *Selected Letters*), and I was entirely convinced by the heart of it. Empson said he "could not possibly complain" about most of what I had said but felt "challenged to defend the treatment of Christianity in my later literary criticism." The draft then takes off into a rather random attack on the Catholic position on birth control and remains unfinished, but before that Empson is clear and concise:

> There has been a total change since my taste was formed, in the twenties, and I did not realise it till I began teaching in England in the fifties. It seemed to me that my pupils had been corrupted into a complete misreading of the literature, and one of a morally disgusting kind; they were continually finding excuses to gloat over the sufferings of someone who was booked for Hell, and they did it with entire complacency, feeling sure that the author had done the same. But he had not. As I was receiving a salary in this line, I would have been taking money on false pretences if I had not complained about the invariable nastiness pretty soon. [SL 601]

I can't say I ever recognized this behavior among my students in England or America, and I doubt whether Empson's students would see themselves in this portrait. But this is only to say that the caricature is extreme, a picture of an attitude that is certainly familiar, if not to be found quite where Empson places it. The moral condition he describes is the one he highlights in the passage we have been looking at in *Milton's God*, where horror is not even recognized as horror; as a voyeuristic pleasure rather, and one licensed by an official culture.

We could apply his analysis to international politics and actual torture, or a moneyed world where corruption will do almost anything but speak its name, and the complicated, self-deceiving mind-set would not change a bit. I think of Jon Stewart's brilliant remark about American interrogations in Iraq: we don't do this kind of thing, even when we are doing it. As Empson's reference to Stalin suggests, he was thinking of the morality of politics as well as theology, and is generally opposed, as Paul Fry reminds us, to "boot-licking admiration" for any sort of tyrant [Fry 38].

But we shall probably hold on to the question most firmly and see its broadest reach if we stay with the vocabulary of hell and damnation and allow it as many meanings, secular and religious, as it will take. We contemplate a group of people, in any century, in heaven or on earth, who see others damned and are not only delighted by the perspective but regard their own delight as virtuous because the best authorities tell them it is. Here we have a whole conspiracy of cruelty: sadism in some, indifference or blind obedience in others, massive self-congratulation all round, and a supposedly benevolent institution wholly in charge.

Or not wholly. The author who had gloated, as the students thought, the institution's yes-man, was the one whose death Barthes proclaimed: he was only a fantasy of the institution itself. The author who had not gloated, as Empson knew, was the one to be found and listened to, even if one almost had to embrace the arguments against the intentional fallacy to do it. Enter John Milton.

II

Milton's intention seems to be clear enough, in and out of *Paradise Lost*, and Empson says we know that a certain speech shows us "Milton's mind at work, because we can relate it to the *De Doctrina*." This claim is not quite as encouraging as it seems, since Empson also tells us that Milton's treatise creates "the effect . . . of a powerful mind thrashing about in exasperation" [MG 136, 115]. From *Seven Types of Ambiguity* onwards, the ever-present author in Empson's criticism can be so divided as not to have anything resembling an intention at all. And here the argument gets more and more interesting. What if God's ways can't be justified? And Milton knows this, at least some of the time? The poem is "not good in spite of but especially because of its moral confusions," and "it is only if you realize what a difficult and unpleasant thing Milton was trying to handle that you can give him his due for the way he handled it" [MG 13, 229].

Milton is "struggling to make his God appear less wicked, as he tells us he will at the start" [MG 11]. There is a small salutary shock in realizing that this is Empson's deadpan paraphrase of the line about justifying God's ways to men, since a whole sinister counter-story hovers in the air. Milton is thinking not that God moves in mysterious ways and that he will do what he can to explain them, but that God is an arch-criminal who needs the best lawyer he can get. Empson doesn't mean to say Milton thinks this consistently, but the effect of his paraphrase is to place the poet somewhere between his own words and Empson's, between fervid faith and dark skepticism. Empson says a "searching goes on in *Paradise Lost*" that constitutes "the chief source of its fascination and poignancy" [MG 11].

Here is Empson's wonderful final defense of Milton:

The root of his power is that he could accept and express a downright horrible conception of God and yet keep somehow alive, underneath it, all the breadth and generosity, the

welcome to every noble pleasure, which had
been prominent in European history just before his time. [MG 276–277]

"Pleasure" is a strange word to use here and seems
to have wandered in from a set of thoughts not
entirely to do with the poem. It suggests that Milton not only represents for Empson an intense
dilemma of faith and argument ("the poem . . .
must be read with growing horror unless you decide to reject its God"; "the reason why the poem
is so good is that it makes God so bad" [MG 25,
275]) but is the inhabitant of a new world: his
own narrow time rather than the old broad open
time. Empson may be remembering the elegiac
thought in *Some Versions of Pastoral,* the speculation that in Satan's "determining to destroy the
innocent happiness of Eden, for the highest political motives, without hatred, not without tears,
we may find some echo of the Elizabethan full-
ness of life that Milton as a poet abandoned, and
as a Puritan helped to destroy" [SV 190–191].

Even Donne is already an inhabitant of this
new time, and in another extraordinary phrase
in the same earlier book Empson describes a
particular poem ("I am a little world") as finally
leaving the reader "safely recalled from the inter-
planetary spaces, baffled among the cramped, inverted, cannibal, appallingly entangled impulses

that are his home upon the world" [SV 76]. His home, and ours. Almost every fantasy Empson has about literal space and mental freedom is contained in this image of a world too small for us. This argument is not really about time, although it looks, with its mention of European history, as if it is; as if we were looking at Empson's version of the dissociation of sensibility, the moment when Humanist curiosity turned into Christian constriction.

But Empson is talking, as he was with his large claims about waste and the human spirit, about the way humans live in any period when institutions, culture or society have them in their grasp, and it is almost dizzying to think he is handsomely praising Milton here for performing the mental trick that was such a problem when believers in the Trinity adopted it. He is not changing his mind, but there is an absence of connective logical tissue—that is what we have to create for ourselves.

As we have seen, Empson is not saying it is wrong to live with unexamined contradictions; we often have to. What's wrong is to turn a contradiction into an alibi, a license to abuse others or ignore their suffering or gloat over it—and feel virtuous while doing such things. This is not Milton's case at all, and he is not even in the end, Empson suggests, either seeking to justify God or to accuse him. He is hoping to conduct a fair trial. If we follow the line of Empson's metaphors closely, Milton defends both or all sides. He does what he can for his "admittedly tricky client God," but also makes as strong a case as he can "for Satan, Eve and Adam." This is because "he could not get under the skin of a character unless he felt he was behaving like a defending counsel" [MG 209, 228].

Isn't it absurd to think of putting God on trial? Yes, if we think of the Godhead as the impersonal order or force behind the universe, or indeed as the chairman of an unruly board of immortals that the Greek Zeus became. But if God is indispensably caught up in a story about fathers and children, if he loves the world as a person would, if he can become incarnate in a human son, then every detail of his story becomes part of the way we imagine him, and many details will allow for different imaginings in different people. The following is something like Empson's literary creed:

> The fundamental purpose of putting elaborate detail into a story is to enable us to use our judgement about the characters; often both their situation and their moral convictions, or their scales of value, are very unlike our own, but we use the detail to imagine how

they feel when they act as they do. . . . Understanding that other people are different is one of the bases of civilization, and this use of a story is as much a culture-conquest as the idea of God. . . . God is on trial, as Professor Diekhoff well remarked; and the reason is that all the characters are on trial in any civilized narrative. [MG 94]

And yet the idea of a trial, fine as the metaphor is for so many works of literature, has a harshness that is not fully part of Empson's view. He doesn't require that Milton conduct the trial in *Paradise Lost*, only that he understand that a trial would be perfectly in order if it were possible. Empson's moral point, always, is not about what we do, but how aware we are of what needs doing, and how hard we try to do it. More, he thinks, cannot be asked of us. Regarding Eliot's dreadful anti-Semitism, for example, he says "a writer had better rise above the ideas of his time, but one should not take offence if he doesn't" [UB 196]. This seems almost lax in its kindness, and yet Empson knows exactly what he is talking about. Of himself, supporting Satan's skepticism about his origin as the creation of God, he writes:

When I was a little boy I was very afraid I might not have the courage which I knew life to demand of me; my life has turned out pretty easy so far, but, if some bully said he would burn me alive unless I pretended to believe he had created me, I hope I would have enough honour to tell him that the evidence did not seem to me decisive. [MG 89]

It would be awful, for his honor, if he turned out not to have the courage, but it would be none of our business to take offense.

Empson can even be relatively kind to God—kinder than we might be if we saw him in the same light. Accepting Aquinas's doctrine that to know in advance that something will happen doesn't mean you made it happen—"this . . . is not beyond our experience"—Empson still thinks that God is on rather dubious ground in his plans for his son: "a parent who 'foresaw' that the children would fall and then insisted upon exposing them to the temptation in view would be considered neurotic, if nothing worse" [MG 116]. This is very mild, and Empson's reading of a famous crux in the poem is even milder. In the prefatory summary to Book V of *Paradise Lost* (the "argument"), Milton says:

God to render man inexcusable sends Raphael to admonish him of his obedience, of his free estate, of his enemy near at hand; who he is, and why his enemy, and whatever else may avail Adam to know.

The standard interpretation of the strange opening phrase ("to render man inexcusable") is that it treats effect as cause, in the way that sentences in the gospels often do. Jesus Christ performs an act, "that the scriptures of the prophets might be fulfilled" [Matthew 26:56], meaning not that this was why he did it, but that when he did, the scriptures were confirmed. God doesn't intend to make man inexcusable, man becomes inexcusable because he doesn't act on the information he is given. However, there are Miltonists who think the phrase means just what it says: God is already sadistically looking forward to the fallen life of his inexcusable creature. Empson calmly says the phrase "might fairly be called a Freudian slip of the tongue" [MG 152]. On Milton's part, he means, but it's engaging to think that God too might be capable of such things.

Empson writes of "the old Protestant" stirring in him, the person who resists almost by instinct the assumption "that a man ought to concur with any herd in which he happens to find himself" [MG 231]. It's the dissenter in Milton that he admires, and at one point he paraphrases Eve's response to God's prohibition regarding the tree of knowledge as that of a conscientious objector: "that you ought not to obey a God if your conscience tells you that his orders are wrong; and that, if your God then sends you to Hell for disobeying him, you were still right to have obeyed your conscience" [MG 160]. Empson isn't saying Milton believes this, or even that Eve is right, only that she has a point. He does recognize the need for obedience in particular cases, and he himself served his country, if not its God, during the war. But obedience is not close to his heart, and the very idea of it is likely to make him think of the herd. Comparing Christianity and Chinese Communism, Empson says he does "recognize that anybody who has experienced either system working well is bound to retain an affection for it, even after coming to realize that it is liable to behave badly." Empson adds, "Still, one needs the realization" [MG 255].

III

Empson's writing on "The Rime of the Ancient Mariner," represented most fully by a 1964 essay and his introduction to *Coleridge's Verse*, is a wild affair, but it helps us to connect his reading of Milton with his late thoughts on Marlowe. The prose is slightly more dated and angry than usual, and has a whiff of the Winchester schoolboy about it. "Come now," he says to us when he thinks we are ready to believe a piece of nonsense [CV 35, 46]. We learn that "the old Coleridge has ratted on the young one," that he "did not discover the meaning till after he had written and then ratted on it as fast as he could" [CV 48, A 305]. There is a lot of snarling about "our current mentors," "our pious critics" and "our modern scolds" [CV 35, 38]. And there is one wonderful moment when Empson insists, not only against Coleridge but also against his own most persuasive argument, that there is no mystery about why the mariner killed the albatross, even though the mariner can scarcely bring himself to talk about the deed. "He shot it for food" [A 300]. Rations often ran short on those long polar voyages.

But Empson's chief claim is intricate and subtle, and his casual manner actually helps its exposition, because it means we have to do quite a bit of construction work ourselves. The poem is about European maritime expansion in the fifteenth and sixteen centuries and the crimes it led to, the slaughter of indigenous peoples in the first instance, and the slave trade at a later moment. The reports of the early journeys of discovery "reek of guilt," Empson says [A 303]. The sailors themselves may not have had the prescience to catch the coming smell, but it surely haunted Coleridge on their behalf. "When, he might ask, will they utter the anguished cry which is basic to the story of the Mariner, 'I did not know it was wrong when I did it?'" [CV 30]. And when will we, who know all about the guilt, stop denying it and offloading it onto religion and superstition? The old crime is the clearly implied basis of the poem, but it doesn't talk about that. It talks about the magical crime of killing a bird, and it converts, especially in its later version, a political story into a harrowing (and of course uplifting) tale of torment and atonement.

This is because the poem's real question, Empson says, is perhaps not "What is the Origin of Evil?" but "Granting there are real grounds for feeling guilty, why are our actual feelings of guilt so bemused and so harmful?" [CV 27]. These actual feelings constitute what Empson calls "Neurotic Guilt": "this is one of the most frequent mental disorders of civilized intelligent mankind, and among literary people it is practically normal" [CV 39]. The disorder takes two forms, or rather, takes one form that can be described in different ways. In the first account, a sense of guilt is accompanied by a strong conviction of innocence—Empson gives several examples. In the second, a sense of guilt is supported by a dogged attribution to the wrong cause. The accounts can also mingle, as when Empson supposes that Coleridge was "feeling that the point where he was innocent had better be made the most of, since he was probably guilty of something else, rather *like* that" [CV 62]. The following suggestion is both shrewd and utterly dizzying: "When Coleridge sounds radiantly innocent he is pretty sure to be lying, or thinking that he is, even if what he says is true" [CV 92]. The sound of innocence is the silence of lying, even when the presumption of lying is false. This is where we remember what is most original and enduring about Empson's writing at its best: the way it follows the velocity of his thought.

If *Milton's God* is about a trial that can't take place, Empson's reading of "The Ancient Mariner" explores our curious longing to be tried for the wrong reason, and to emerge from the process "sadder and wiser," as the poem's Wedding-Guest is at the end of the Mariner's narration. Empson says this conclusion "still puts my teeth on edge" (CV 80), but he recognizes that it too is an important aspect of the delusion. We might think that *Doctor Faustus*, the object of Empson's last major work of criticism, would put these concerns to rest. A man sells his soul to the devil and the devil collects. Where is the injustice or displacement in that? One answer is that no one could possibly deserve the torments Christianity designs for the damned, and this is part of Empson's case. But he has other tricks up his sleeve.

IV

Empson's story of what he thinks happened to the text of Marlowe's *Doctor Faustus* makes almost all other conspiracy theories seem timid. Still, there is plenty of room for speculation. Marlowe was killed in 1594, the year in which performances of his play are first recorded. There is every reason to believe the play had been staged well before that, perhaps as early as 1589. The first published text of the play did not appear until 1604; another, slightly longer text appeared in 1616. For quite a while scholars preferred the second text as the more authentic; recently they have turned to the first. Empson is sure the second was rewritten by someone other than Marlowe because of its "insistence . . . upon sending Faust to a real Hell," and its "sniggering sadism near the end" [FC 44], but also believes that the first text is a long way from representing the play Marlowe initially wrote.

Empson worked on his book *Faustus and the Censor* during the last ten years of his life, and did not complete a final version. The published text of 1987, although shaped in various ways by its editor, John Henry Jones, contains only Empson's words, apart from a hundred or so added for linking passages. Empson's theory is that the play as first performed did not end in Faustus's damnation. Departing from the moralism of its English and German sources, it told the rakish, dangerous story of a trickster rather than the severe tale of a condemned Satanist. All the comic scenes seem to confirm this reading, and the only problem is how a man who sold his soul to the devil could manage not to pay the price when his time came. Prior, that is, to Goethe's romantic theory that striving itself, whether for good or ill, is enough to save a man. Or the desperate delusion of the hero of Thomas Mann's Faust novel, who tries to believe that having made things hard for himself might bring him closer to forgiveness.

Empson's answer is that Marlowe, an intellectual and an atheist, would know that he couldn't get away with saving the Faustus of the infernal bargain but would also not want to punish such a brave and irreverent fellow. "He really would feel bitterly ashamed, on high moral grounds, if he knew that just after his death his play was being twisted into recommending eternal torture" [FC 41]. Fortunately, Marlowe had a recourse in a popular belief of the time. Angels and demons existed, but so did fairies and all kinds of other supernatural creatures, including a set called middle spirits. They belonged neither to heaven nor to hell, but were not entirely of this earth either, since in many cases they lived for a thousand years or so. Empson plausibly suggests that the idea of such spirits was attractive to scholars at the time because they could include the pagan gods in such a category. They didn't all have to become devils in Greek disguise, as they were in Milton. The Church denied the existence of middle spirits, but apparently never declared the belief in them a heresy, and a theatre audience could think what it liked—for a while. As Fry intriguingly suggests, "Middle Spirits . . . are the energy of Dissent" [Fry 145]. In Empson's reading, Mephistopheles is such a spirit, and the play becomes a huge romp through dreams of infinite power and many deceptions. Faustus "is an avatar of the demigod rogue, found in practically all ancient literatures and surviving oral cultures—the ideal drinking companion, the great fixer, who can break taboos for you and get away with it" [FC 46–47]. He dies at the end, of course, but he doesn't go to hell—or to heaven, because "having become legally a Middle Spirit," as Empson put it in a lecture, he would be "entitled to oblivion," to the comparative calm of dying like an animal [FC 2]. It is true that the first clause of Faustus's signed pact with the supposed Devil requires that he "may be a spirit in form and substance," without specifying what sort of spirit he is to be.

This, Empson says, was the play the first audiences watched, and of which we can now read only fragments. Then the censor saw it or heard of it and banned it. The fact of this intervention "should have been plain" to us, Empson says, "but our political innocence kept us from seeing it."

He makes the same point more grimly when he says "the disastrous changes in the modern world, often returning to earlier conditions, should have at least one good effect; historians may now understand better what happened under a Thought Police" [FC 44, 53]. After the censor's action there were only correctional rewrites, with Faustus securely put in his place and properly punished. Nothing unorthodox any more, except the spectacular verse of Faustus's desire for dia-bolical knowledge, and of course Mephistopheles' horrifyingly eloquent and sophisticated account of the nature of hell. Mephistopheles knows as well as his disciple Satan in *Paradise Lost* that hell is not a place, and Faustus soon learns the same. Mephistopheles also knows, and is no doubt the source of, Empson's earlier poetic theory of the "last pain" of the damned:

> Why this is hell, nor am I out of it.
> Think'st thou that I, who saw the face of God,
> And tasted the eternal joys of heaven,
> Am not tormented with ten thousand hells
> In being deprived of everlasting bliss?

The intricate twist in Empson's imagined un-censored version is that the atheist Faustus still fears hell, and Mephistopheles plays upon this fear—so that quite a few scenes in the published text make good sense as they are—but the fear is finally banished and the hellish pretense ends. Here is Empson's dazzling account of what he says is "the original story." He calls his spirit Meph in order not to get caught up in the quarrels about different spellings in different texts (-istopheles, -ostophilis, -astophilis), although he does also say that Mephistopheles is "the best form of the name."

Marlowe supposes a Middle Spirit who is a quisling or rather a double agent, professing to work for the devils, and actually inducing them to grant their powers to Faust, but on condition that Faust gives his immortal soul beforehand to the quisling. Faust is at first delighted by the results but before long the intense experience becomes too much for his nerves; he decides to repent, supposing he may yet go to Heaven. Meph regards this as a cheat and counters it by saying that he really is a devil, so that Faust has really sold his soul. To prove it he calls up the Devil and his whole court, at the end of Act II (they are a charade put on by his Middle Spirit friends). Faust, after a brief crisis of horror, decides to live bravely for his time on earth. . . . But at the end, when Meph has succeeded in bringing him to the agreed hour of death without having repented, so that Meph gets his immortal soul, nothing happens except that his old friend advances upon him with open arms and a broad smile. The last two words of Faust are "Ah Mephastophilis," and the censor could not rule how the actor was to speak them. He dies in the arms of his deceitful friend with immense relief, also gratitude, surprise, love, forgiveness, and exhaustion. It is the happiest death in all drama. [FC 121–122]

This is a wonderful tale, especially when we remember there is no extra-literary evidence at all for its ever having been told till now ("the best evidence for this theory of the play is that it gives point and thrust to so many of the details" [FC 123]), but it is open to one serious objection even as a fiction. Is a man who hopes to gain knowledge and power without paying the devil's price, because he thinks he has found a third party who can deliver the same goods at less extravagant cost, as interesting as a man who really will give his soul in order to know what no other human knows and to do what no other human can do? It's true that there are moments when the familiar Faustus seems to doubt the existence of hell and the devil, so he may believe he can somehow enjoy the real winnings of an imaginary wager, but this is a tragic illusion. It is also true that Empson's Faustus is not sure, for much of the play, that Mephistopheles is not a devil; he can only hope, and everything Mephistopheles does is meant to prove his hope groundless. "His terrors deserve every sympathy," Empson says. "I am not making the play trivial" [FC 194].

I think we can grant that Empson's reading is not trivial. The suspense created by the running anxiety and fraud is too great for that. But the gap between the revealed comedy and the concluded tragedy, between Empson's reading of the words "Ah Mephastophilis" ("you rascal, you were lying all along") and the familiar one ("we've been through so much together, but finally you're a devil and I'm a man") is so large that it becomes more important than either story taken on its own. Empson's creation of this new/old play shifts the center of the argument in another way too, making his Faustus book the perfect complement to *Milton's God*. For a brief and probably imaginary moment Marlowe undoes the Christian devotion to torture, and Faustus's escape from hell is not only a happy ending for him but a defeat of God's ogrish appetite for victims.

"I alone know the plan of this savage sideshow." Empson's borrowing of Rimbaud's boast comes to mind again. Perhaps it doesn't matter that only Empson knows the plan of this ultimately less than savage Faustian spectacle, since he shared his secret with us in so much eloquent detail. Do we believe the theory, the story of the lost and rescued play? As with so much of Empson's later writing, it's hard to imagine that he is offering it to us as history. He is, though, because as we have seen he thinks fiction is an acceptable road to fact if no other road will take us there. We may read him with some skepticism, but only about his claim for a literal final result. If Marlowe didn't invent the happiest death in all drama, Empson did, and in the act, in the writing, invited us to think again about happiness, death and drama in ways we couldn't have managed without him.

▨ ACKNOWLEDGMENTS

Thanks to Alison McKeen for thinking of this book; to Anne Savarese for making it happen; to Jodi Beder for subtle and intelligent editing; to Mary-Kay Wilmers and Robert Silvers for encouragements ancient and modern; to Susan Wolfson for some wonderful conversations; to my students and colleagues at Princeton and Bread Loaf for wit and company; and to Ava Turner, who always knows when to laugh.

⬢ ABBREVIATIONS

Works cited have been identified in the text by the following abbreviations.

BOOKS BY EMPSON

A	*Argufying*. Iowa City: University of Iowa Press, 1987
CP	*The Complete Poems of William Empson*. London: Penguin, 2001
CV	*Coleridge's Verse*. New York: Schocken Books, 1973
CW	*The Structure of Complex Words*. Ann Arbor: University of Michigan Press, 1967
ES	*Essays on Shakespeare*. Cambridge: Cambridge University Press, 1986
FB	*The Face of the Buddha*. Oxford: Oxford University Press, 2016
FC	*Faustus and the Censor*. Oxford: Basil Blackwell, 1987
MG	*Milton's God*. London: Chatto & Windus, 1965
RL1	*Essays on Renaissance Literature*, vol. 1. Cambridge: Cambridge University Press, 1993

RL2   *Essays on Renaissance Literature*, vol. 2. Cambridge: Cambridge University Press, 1994

SL   *Selected Letters*. Oxford: Oxford University Press, 2009

SS   *The Strengths of Shakespeare's Shrew*. Sheffield: Sheffield Academic Press, 1996

ST   *Seven Types of Ambiguity*. New York: New Directions, 1966

SV   *Some Versions of Pastoral*. New York: New Directions, 1974

UB   *Using Biography*. London: Chatto & Windus, 1984

WORKS BY OTHERS

Cameron   Sharon Cameron, "Introduction by Way of William Empson's Buddha Faces," in *Impersonality: Seven Essays*. Chicago: University of Chicago Press, 2007

Fry   Paul Fry, *William Empson: Prophet against Sacrifice*. London: Routledge, 1991

Gardner   Philip Gardner and Averil Gardner, *The God Approached: A Commentary on the Poems of William Empson*. Totowa, NJ: Rowman & Littlefield, 1978

Haffenden I   John Haffenden, *William Empson: Among the Mandarins*. Oxford and New York: Oxford University Press, 2005

Haffenden II   John Haffenden, *William Empson: Against the Christians*. Oxford and New York: Oxford University Press, 2006

Norris   Christopher Norris, *William Empson and the Philosophy of Literary Criticism*. London: Athlone, 1978

Reid   David Stuart Reid, *Ambiguities: Conflict and Union of Opposites in Robert Graves, Laura Riding, William Empson and Yvor Winters*. Bethesda, MD: Academica Press, 2012

Ricks   Christopher Ricks, "Empson's Poetry," in Roma Gill,
       ed., *William Empson: The Man and His Work*. London:
       Routledge and Kegan Paul, 1974

Righter   William Righter, *The Myth of Theory*. Cambridge:
       Cambridge University Press, 1984

❖ BIBLIOGRAPHY

I. WORKS BY EMPSON

Seven Types of Ambiguity. London: Chatto & Windus, 1930.

Some Versions of Pastoral. London: Chatto & Windus, 1935.

Poems. London: Chatto & Windus, 1935.

The Gathering Storm. London: Faber and Faber, 1940.

Collected Poems. New York: Harcourt, Brace, 1949.

The Structure of Complex Words. London: Chatto & Windus, 1951; Ann Arbor: University of Michigan Press, 1967.

Milton's God. London: Chatto & Windus, 1961.

[Edited with David Pirie] *Coleridge's Verse: A Selection*. London: Faber, 1972; New York: Schocken Books, 1973.

Using Biography. London: Chatto & Windus, 1984.

Essays on Shakespeare. Cambridge: Cambridge University Press, 1986.

The Royal Beasts and Other Works. Iowa City: University of Iowa Press, 1988.

Argufying: Essays on Literature and Culture. Iowa City: University of Iowa Press, 1987.

Faustus and the Censor: The English Faust-Book and Marlowe's Doctor Faustus. Oxford: Blackwell, 1987.

Essays on Renaissance Literature, vol. 1. Cambridge: Cambridge University Press, 1993.

Essays on Renaissance Literature, vol. 2. Cambridge: Cambridge University Press, 1994.

The Strengths of Shakespeare's Shrew: Essays, Memoirs, and Reviews. Sheffield: Sheffield Academic Press, 1996.

The Complete Poems of William Empson. John Haffenden, ed. Hardmondsworth: Penguin, 2001.

Selected Letters. John Haffenden, ed. Oxford: Oxford University Press, 2006.

The Face of the Buddha. Rupert Arrowsmith, ed. Oxford: Oxford University Press, 2016.

II. WORKS ABOUT EMPSON

Bevis, Matthew, ed. *Some Versions of Empson.* Oxford and New York: Oxford University Press, 2007.

Cameron, Sharon. "Introduction by Way of William Empson's Buddha Faces." In *Impersonality: Seven Essays.* Chicago: University of Chicago Press, 2007.

Childs, Donald J. *The Birth of New Criticism: Conflict and Conciliation in the Early Work of William Empson, I. A. Richards, Laura Riding, and Robert Graves.* Montreal: McGill-Queen's University Press, 2013.

Constable, John, ed. *Critical Essays on William Empson.* Aldershot, Brookfield: Ashgate, 1993.

Donoghue, Denis. "Some Versions of Empson." *Times Literary Supplement,* June, 7, 1974.

Empson, Jacob. *Hetta and William: A Memoir of a Bohemian Marriage.* Bloomington, IN: AuthorHouse, 2012.

Fry, Paul. *William Empson: Prophet against Sacrifice.* London: Routledge, 1991.

Gardner, Philip, and Averil Gardner. *The God Approached: A Commentary on the Poems of William Empson.* Totowa, NJ: Rowman & Littlefield, 1978.

Gill, Roma, and Moira Megaw, eds. *William Empson: The Man and His Work*. London: Routledge & Kegan Paul, 1974.

Grady, Hugh, ed. *Empson, Wilson Knight, Barber, Kott*. London and New York: Continuum, 2012.

Gunn, Thom. "Empson's Collected Poems." *London Magazine*, February 1, 1956.

Haffenden, John. *William Empson: Against the Christians*. Oxford and New York: Oxford University Press, 2006.

Haffenden, John. *William Empson: Among the Mandarins*. Oxford and New York: Oxford University Press, 2005.

Hertz, Neil. "More Lurid Figures: De Man Reading Empson." In Norris and Mapp, eds., *William Empson: The Critical Achievement*.

Norris, Christopher. *William Empson and the Philosophy of Literary Criticism*. London: Athlone, 1978.

Norris, Christopher, and Nigel Mapp, eds. *William Empson: The Critical Achievement*. Cambridge and New York: Cambridge University Press, 1993.

Perry, Seamus. "Coleridge, William Empson and Japan." In *Coleridge, Romanticism and the Orient*, ed. David Vallins, Kaz Oishi and Seamus Perry. London: Bloomsbury, 2013.

Price, Katy. *Loving Faster than Light: Romance and Readers in Einstein's Universe*. Chicago and London: University of Chicago Press, 2012.

Reid, David Stuart. *Ambiguities: Conflict and Union of Opposites in Robert Graves, Laura Riding, William Empson and Yvor Winters*. Bethesda, MD: Academica Press, 2012.

Ricks, Christopher. *Allusion to the Poets*. Oxford: Oxford University Press, 2004.

Ricks, Christopher, "Empson's Poetry." In Roma Gill and Moira Megaw, eds., *William Empson: The Man and His Work*. London: Routledge and Kegan Paul, 1974.

Ricks, Christopher. *The Force of Poetry*. Oxford: Clarendon Press, 1995.

Righter, William. *The Myth of Theory*. Cambridge: Cambridge University Press, 1984.

Sale, Roger. *Modern Heroism: Essays on D.H. Lawrence, William Empson, and J.R.R. Tolkien*. Berkeley and London: University of California Press, 1973.

Wain, John. *Preliminary Essays*. London and New York: Macmillan, St. Martin's, 1957.

Willis, J. H. *William Empson*. New York: Columbia University Press, 1969.

III. OTHER RELATED WORKS

Adorno, T. W. "The Essay as Form." In *Notes to Literature*, vol. 1. Rolf Tiedemann, ed.; Shierry Weber Nicholsen, trans. New York: Columbia University Press, 1991.

Austin, J. L. *Philosophical Papers*. Oxford: Clarendon Press, 1990.

Barthes, Roland. *Critique et vérité*, Paris: Editions du Seuil, 1966.

Barthes, Roland. "La mort de l'auteur." In *Le bruissement de la langue*. Paris: Editions du Seuil, 1984.

Barthes, Roland. *Le plaisir du texte*. Paris: Seuil, 1973.

Best, Stephen, and Sharon Marcus. "Surface Reading: An Introduction." *Representations* 108 (Fall 2009).

Bishop, Elizabeth. "One Art." In *Poems*. New York: Farrar, Straus and Giroux, 2011.

Blackmur, R. P. "A Critic's Job of Work." In *Selected Essays*. New York: Ecco Press, 1986.

Bronte, Emily. *Wuthering Heights*, p. 337. Harmondsworth: Penguin, 2002.

Brooks, Cleanth. "Hits and Misses." *Kenyon Review* 14 (1952).

Carroll, Lewis. *Alice's Adventures in Wonderland and Through the Looking-Glass*. New York: Bantam, 1984.

Chomsky, Noam. *Language and Mind*, p. 61. Cambridge: Cambridge University Press, 2006.

Donne, John. "A Nocturnal upon St Lucy's Day." In *The Complete English Poems*, ed. A. J. Smith. Harmondsworth: Penguin, 1977.

Eliot, T. S. "The Love Song of J. Alfred Prufrock." In *Collected Poems*. New York: Harcourt Brace Jovanovich, 1991.

Eliot, T. S. "The Metaphysical Poets." In *Selected Prose*, ed. Frank Kermode. London: Faber and Faber, 1975.

Freud, Sigmund. *On Dreams*. New York: Norton, 1990.

Hopkins, Gerard Manley. "Pied Beauty" ("Glory be to God for dappled things"). In *The Major Works*. Oxford: Oxford University Press, 2009.

James, Henry. *The Art of the Novel*. Chicago: Chicago University Press, 2011.

James, Henry. "The Jolly Corner." In *The Complete Stories*. New York: Library of America, 1996.

Kermode, Frank. "The heart of standing is you cannot fly." *London Review of Books*, June 22, 2000.

Miller, David A. "Hitchcock's Hidden Pictures." *Critical Inquiry* 37:1 (Autumn 2010).

Milton, John. "L'Allegro" ("Till the dappled dawn doth rise"). In *The Complete Poems*. Harmondsworth: Penguin, 1999.

Moretti, Franco. *Distant Reading*. London and New York: Verso, 2013.

Rimbaud, Arthur. *Illuminations*. Trans. John Ashbery. Manchester: Carcanet, 2011.

Shakespeare, William. *King Lear*. New York: Modern Library, 2009.

Williams, C. K. "Villanelle of the Suicide's Mother." In *Collected Poems*. New York: Farrar, Straus and Giroux, 2011.

Wimsatt, W. K., and Monroe C. Beardsley. "The Intentional Fallacy." In *The Verbal Icon*. Louisville: University Press of Kentucky.

Wittgenstein, Ludwig. *Tractatus Logico-Philosophicus*. London: Routledge, 1974.

Yeats, W. B. "The Phases of the Moon." In *Collected Works*, vol. 1. New York: Scribner, 1997.